INTERNATIONAL MONETARY COOPERATION AMONG THE UNITED STATES, JAPAN, AND GERMANY

INTERNATIONAL MONETARY COOPERATION AMONG THE UNITED STATES, JAPAN, AND GERMANY

by

KEISUKE IIDA
Princeton University

KLUWER ACADEMIC PUBLISHERS

BOSTON / DORDRECHT / LONDON

Distributors for North, Central and South America:
Kluwer Academic Publishers
101 Philip Drive
Assinippi Park
Norwell, Massachusetts 02061 USA
Telephone (781) 871-6600
Fax (781) 871-6528
E-Mail <kluwer@wkap.com>

Distributors for all other countries:
Kluwer Academic Publishers Group
Distribution Centre
Post Office Box 322
3300 AH Dordrecht, THE NETHERLANDS
Telephone 31 78 6392 392
Fax 31 78 6546 474
E-Mail <orderdept@wkap.nl>

 Electronic Services <http://www.wkap.nl>

Library of Congress Cataloging-in-Publication Data
Iida, Keisuke.
   International monetary cooperation among the United States, Japan,
and Germany / by Keisuke Iida.
            p.   cm.
   Includes index.
   ISBN 0-7923-8459-8
   1. International finance.   2. Monetary policy--International
cooperation.   3. Monetary policy--United States.   4. Monetary
policy--Japan.   5. Monetary policy--Germany.   I. Title.
HG3881.I32   1999
332'.045--dc21   98-52217
                                                     CIP

Printed on acid-free paper.

Printed in the United States of America

JK

To Ruthie

Contents

Tables

Figures

Preface

This work offers a first—and overdue—book-length study of counterproductive cooperation. Students of international cooperation tend to assume that cooperation is desirable in principle yet difficult in practice. But actual policymakers, for their part, are far from convinced that cooperation is always desirable. Indeed, in monetary affairs, it is almost always contested. Partly reflecting their sentiment, the idea that international monetary cooperation can often be counterproductive has become influential of late especially among economists. If proved to be true, this idea poses a very serious challenge to the academic study of international cooperation, which has burgeoned over the past two decades or so. Thus, it is critical for us to understand why and under what conditions monetary cooperation can be counterproductive rather than beneficial. For the first time, this book presents all the theories of counterproductive cooperation in one place, subjects them to systematic, empirical scrutiny in light of the experience of G-3 (U.S., German, and Japanese) cooperation since the 1970s, and suggests policy recommendations in light of the findings.

Specifically, the book classifies the theories of counterproductive monetary cooperation into four groups—third-party (or market expectations) effects, perverse incentives, model uncertainty, and international coercion. Although it finds support for all of them, the theory of model uncertainty, originally proposed by Jeffrey Frankel, is shown to be most enlightening and robust. Frankel's theory says essentially that the economic knowledge of monetary policymakers is just not precise enough to be a reliable guide for beneficial and risk-free cooperation; it is a roadmap fraught with such margins of error that cooperation could easily lead to serious policy error. Furthermore, the theory has some predictable behavioral consequences. First, policymakers, in proposing different interpretations of events (whether successful or not) both before and after cooperation, often find themselves trapped in acrimonious debate. Second, if policymakers or other observers come away having learned that cooperation did not pay off, they will have less incentive to cooperate thenceforth. I am particularly concerned about this last consequence: I nevertheless believe that there are situations in which cooperation is essential, despite the constraints imposed by model uncertainty.

As for the other theories of counterproductive cooperation, Kenneth Rogoff, for example, makes a forceful argument that if monetary policy has an inflationary bias (i.e., a tendency to produce higher inflation than is socially optimal), international cooperation can seriously exacerbate that bias. I find some support for this theory, but not as much as for Frankel's.

Yet another group of theories holds that if policymakers begin with some perverse (i.e., socially undesirable) incentives, international cooperation can aggravate the pernicious consequences of policy. Guido Tabellini, for example, shows that budget deficits can increase under a regime of fiscal policy coordination if politicians are myopic due to elections.

Finally, political scientists have their own favorite alternative explanation: a realist theory of international relations, which predicts that international "cooperation" may not be beneficial if one state coerces another into submission in the name of cooperation. Monetary policy authorities are fond of "technical" monetary policy making and hence wary of politicizing monetary policy. For better or for worse, attempts at international monetary cooperation tend to become highly politicized, as politicians get directly involved because they feel that "business as usual" is not working. Thus, central banks perceive that their political independence is threatened; their subjective payoff goes down; if they react with some policy that is not calculated optimally, the resulting policy outcome could be counterproductive for society as a whole.

The book moves on to examine another area of cooperation among the G3 central banks: coordination of foreign exchange intervention, which occurs with more frequency than monetary and fiscal policy coordination. A number of economists argue that such intervention is highly ineffective and that coordination does nothing to improve on that ineffectiveness. A few economists go so far as to argue that foreign exchange intervention is counterproductive because it can in fact destabilize markets despite the purported aim of accomplishing the opposite.

The empirical evidence presented in this book is far-reaching and complex. It shows overall that although there is some support for all of the above theories, it is hard to establish a firm link between coordination (or their underlying factors) and the explained consequences that are claimed to be counterproductive. Although there is some evidence, for example, that periods of monetary coordination are associated with faster monetary growth, as predicted by Rogoff, the average inflation rates in coordination periods are not actually notably higher than in noncoordination years. The reason is simple: uncoordinated monetary policy can be just as inflationary as coordinated monetary policy, and therefore, the inflationary bias of coordination is not particularly notable.

This leads us back to the simple fact that the outcomes of cooperation may or may not be particularly different from those of noncooperation, which is, again, highly consistent with the theory of model uncertainty. Whenever other theories fail empirically, the theory of model uncertainty receives support.

Intellectual purists and deterministic theorists scorn such an ambiguous theory; indeed, Albert Einstein detested the uncertainty principle in quantum physics. Rather, policymakers evince enormous confidence in their unshakable belief either that monetary cooperation is beneficial or conversely that it is indisputably counterproductive. It is the theory of uncertainty—just like the uncertainty principle—that remains valid as far as international monetary cooperation is concerned, and its policy implications are immense. Consequently, I argue (1) that uncertainty needs to be studied more systematically in the policy-relevant settings rather than just at think tanks, (2) that international monetary cooperation needs careful planning that takes full account of the effects of such uncertainty, (3) that hedging and diversification in the policy "portfolio" is warranted, (4) that policymakers train with psychologists in coping with uncertainty, and (5) that policymakers should be courageous enough to give cooperation a chance when and only when the possible consequences of noncooperation are immense and the possible costs of counterproductive cooperation controllable.

This book is organized as follows. Chapter 1 explains the importance of international monetary cooperation among the major economic powers of today's world and then presents the major theories of counterproductive cooperation informally. Chapter 2 elaborates on these theories. Chapter 3 presents both quantitative and qualitative evidence pertaining to these theories of counterproductive monetary (and fiscal) policy coordination. Chapter 4 adds some more theories on the ineffectiveness and counterproductiveness of concerted foreign exchange intervention and presents both quantitative and qualitative evidence. Chapter 5 summarizes the findings, draws the implications of these findings, and presents policy recommendations.

A few words about the intended audience of this book are in order. Originally, because of the highly technical nature of the material, I had thought in terms of a readership of experts on international finance in economics and students of international political economy. In light of the importance of the subject matter, however, I have decided to address a wider audience. Thus, it is my hope that students of international cooperation in trade and security fields will find the book both informative and enlightening, that students in economics interested in how abstract mathematics plays out in the real world may find the case studies interesting, and that those professionally and privately concerned with what the Fed is up to may rediscover the simple truth that there is no real divide between economics and politics, even in this seemingly technical field.

Acknowledgements

This book would not have been possible without support from a number of friends and colleagues. In particular, I would like to thank Bob Keohane and Bob Putnam for starting me on this path in graduate school. Although this book bears almost no resemblance to my doctoral dissertation from which it originated, I hope I have still kept many of their insights herein. A number of people have read and commented on successive versions of the manuscript. I would like to thank Mike Doyle, Joanne Gowa, Kate McNamara, and Beth Simmons, in particular, for their friendly criticisms from which this book greatly benefited. I cannot thank Jaliya Stewart enough for her competent and painstaking research assistance. Ilene Cohen has copy-edited the manuscript with high professionalism. Without editing support from Ranak Jasani, Paul Kalkman, and Yana Lambert, this book would not have seen the light of day. Last but not least, I would like to thank Ruthie, Clayton, and Ellen for putting up with me all these years when the book seemed more important than the family.

Keisuke Iida

Princeton, New Jersey

Chapter 1

Introduction

1. INTRODUCTION

No sensible person would choose to study it [international cooperation] as a topic of investigation on the grounds that its puzzles could be readily "solved." I study it ... because of its normative significance. Robert O. Keohane, *After Hegemony*.

We study international monetary cooperation because of the importance of international monetary and financial stability, and cooperation is known to be one of the major ways to promote stability. The current financial crisis in Asia reminds us once again how fragile the international monetary system is and how susceptible to shocks and contagion. Bubbles in real estate markets in Thailand burst in the summer of 1997, and many financial institutions collapsed. Fearful of further financial turmoil, foreign money fled the country, and the currency was battered. The crisis soon spread to the nearby countries in Southeast Asia, enveloping Indonesia, the Philippines, and Malaysia, forcing all to abandon their peg to either the dollar or a basket of foreign currencies. Malaysia's prime minister, Dr. Mahathir Mohamad, found his scapegoat quickly: he accused George Soros—the noted American financier—of conspiring to ruin the economic success story of what the World Bank had dubbed as miracle economies only a few years before. Responding to the gravity of the situation, the International Monetary Fund (IMF) and Japan quickly extended emergency loans to Thailand and Indonesia, but the crisis was still not readily contained. By November, it spread to South Korea, another miracle economy, which had already been brought to its knees by the financial mismanagement in many of its conglomerates earlier in the year. Facing a presidential election in December, Korea was reluctant to tarnish its pristine image by asking for a bailout. Eventually, the Korean government bowed to market pressures and went begging at the IMF, which granted an unprecedented $57 billion package. The Asian crisis continued unabated in 1998. Under the pressure of political turmoil set off by the IMF-led reform, the 32-year-long Suharto regime fell in May. Somewhat independently, Russia fell into crisis in August, defaulting on its debt and letting the rouble devalue by half. As of this writing, the crisis is threatening to spread to Latin America.

This recent course of events underscores Kindleberger's thesis that bubbles and ensuing panics are very common in finance.[1] Furthermore, these financial crises often take on an international dimension, as investors not only rush to pull their money out of the country in crisis but also try to get their capital out of other countries that have extensive economic ties to the former. For instance, a small crisis in Austria in 1931 spread to Germany and then to Britain, eventually to bring down the gold standard; presumably this was the dynamic at play in Asia in 1997 as well.

More often than not, these financial crises are self-fulfilling prophesies: once enough people begin to doubt a country's creditworthiness, capital flees so fast that the country inevitably finds itself in a liquidity crisis, even if the fundamentals are relatively sound. In such a case official intervention is needed to calm frightened investors. In a domestic context, there are already two major mechanisms in place: deposit insurance and the lender-of-last-resort function performed by the central bank. Deposit insurance prevents a panic in the first place by guaranteeing depositors that they can recover their money if a depository institution fails. Furthermore, if the central bank injects liquidity into the ailing institution, acting as a lender of last resort, an imminent collapse of the institution may be forestalled. While there is no precise global analogue to deposit insurance, emergency loans extended by the Bank for International Settlements (BIS), the IMF, and major industrial societies such as the United States are international equivalents of lenders of last resort.

Kindleberger firmly believes in the need for a single dominant financial player in the world—what other scholars call "hegemony"—that can serve in effect as an international lender of last resort: "[F]or the world economy to be stabilized, there has to be a stabilizer, one stabilizer."[2] The hegemon's role is not limited to emergency lending, however. A stabilizer will "provide a market for distress goods [and] a steady if not countercyclical flow of capital; it would also manage, in some degree, the structure of foreign exchange rates and provide a degree of coordination of domestic monetary policies."[3] In sum, hegemony is essential for maintaining a modicum of stability when the international financial system is in panic.

Indeed, according to Kindleberger, hegemony is the only way to impart stability to the otherwise unstable world of global finance. From early on, however, another approach to maintaining stability suggested itself as an alternative: international monetary cooperation. Kindleberger summarily rejects it as an effective route: "With a duumvirate, a troika, or slightly wider forms of collective responsibility, the buck has no place to stop."[4]

Kindleberger insists that a stabilizer be the monetary authorities of a single dominant country. An international institution such as the IMF would not be enough, because as he sees it, international institutions are merely reflections of the fractional collectivity of member governments. They suffer from the collective action or free-riding problem as well as inevitable sluggishness of an oversized bureaucracy. At best, "regimes [i.e., international lending institutions] work well in best times, but something more in the way of leadership is called for in crisis."[5]

Hegemony is not without problems of its own, however. First, there may be no natural candidate for a leader in the international economy. Thus, for example, American economic prominence has declined, and no other leader is clearly in sight. Are we therefore resigned to increasing instability during the interregnum? Perhaps not. It may be that international cooperation and institutions may hold out some hope in the absence of hegemony.[6] Second, even when a single dominant economy exists on the world scene, its government or central bank may not be willing to take on the challenge of international leadership. Such was the case with the United States in the interwar period.

Barry Eichengreen has examined the track record of both hegemonic leadership and cooperation as alternative methods of providing international financial stability and concluded that cooperation wins hands down.[7] His findings are summarized in Table 1.1. Eichengreen compared three essential functions of the well-functioning international monetary system—provision of international liquidity, adjustment of domestic economies, and international lenders of last resort—in three different periods. He found that the notion of British hegemony tended to be exaggerated: it was often a "borrower of last resort" and the Bank of England relied on cooperation from France, Germany, and Russia in many important international crises.[8] In short, cooperation was crucial even in the heyday of British financial primacy. Furthermore, Eichengreen also differs from Kindleberger in his interpretation of the moral of the interwar period. Cooperation provided a degree of stability during the 1920s. It was only in the 1930s that the international monetary system became exceedingly unstable, eventually resulting in the collapse of the gold standard, but that was the result of various diplomatic disputes interfering with effective cooperation among major European central banks.[9] Therefore, Eichengreen concludes, "the international monetary system has always been 'after hegemony' in the sense that more than a dominant economic power was required to ensure the provision and maintenance of international monetary stability."[10]

Table 1.1. **Historical evidence of leadership and cooperation**

	Leadership	Cooperation
Classical gold standard (1870s-1914)		
Adjustment	Bank of England as "conductor of international orchestra"	Collective hegemony of Europe
Lender of last resort	Bank of England as lender of last resort	Bank of England often "borrower of last resort"
Interwar period (1919-39)		
Liquidity	Britain persuades other countries to supplement gold with sterling	Genoa conference partly resolves the problem
Adjustment	Bank of England no longer "conductor"	Increasing role of internal conditions
Lender of last resort	Band of England no longer lender of last resort	Diplomatic disputes impede cooperation
Bretton Woods (1944-71)		
Liquidity	U.S. dollar as liquidity backed by gold	Non-U.S. governments willing to hold on to dollar to maintain the system
Adjustment	IMF (backed by U.S.) as conductor	U.S. unable to adjust
Lender of last resort	U.S. as lender of last resort	International crisis lending mostly cooperative

2. THE FLOAT AND MONETARY UNION

It could be argued, however, that Eichengreen's findings are limited because he focused exclusively on fixed exchange rate systems such as the classical gold standard, the interwar gold-exchange standard, and the Bretton Woods system. Fixed exchange rate regimes are notoriously prone to speculative attacks when the markets suspect that currency devaluation is imminent. A government trying to defend a currency peg from speculative attacks essentially offers a one-way bet. By selling the currency under pressure, speculators lose nothing if devaluation does not occur, and they make a fortune if devaluation materializes. By contrast, when a currency is free to move in either direction as in a flexible exchange rate regime, speculation can be stabilizing because speculators can make profits only by buying low and selling high.[11] Milton Friedman argued persuasively that flexible exchange rates do not necessarily mean greater instability than fixed ones: "A flexible exchange rate need not be an unstable exchange rate. If it is, it is primarily because there is underlying instability in the economic conditions governing international trade. And a rigid exchange rate may, while itself nominally stable, perpetuate and accentuate other elements of instability in the economy."[12]

Pace Friedman, however, the experience of the floating rates among the major currencies since 1973 has not been terribly sanguine. Worldwide inflation in the 1970s and the dollar's roller-coaster ride in the 1980s seemed to indicate, at least on the surface, that the float is not a panacea, even if it is also not the unmitigated disaster that doomsayers may have suggested. Friedman was certainly right that flexibility helps alleviate balance-of-payments imbalances in the medium term. But, as the experience of the United States and the U.K. shows, it is not enough to eliminate all the imbalances. Exchange crises can still occur when some currencies sharply depreciate in a short period of time. Major financial institutions could fail in the course of speculative currency trading, as the Franklin National of New York and Bankhaus I.D. Herstatt of Cologne did in 1974. Thus, the need for a fix such as international cooperation may still remain even under a flexible exchange rate system.

Indeed, most developing countries, which are very susceptible to capital flight and exchange crises, continued to peg their currencies to the dollar and other key currencies after 1973. But more recently they have been gradually departing from a peg. In 1984, for instance, as many as 62.5 percent of currencies in the world were pegged, while ten years later the proportion of pegged currencies had declined to 38.9 percent.[13] This is because financial integration increased capital mobility, which makes it difficult to fix exchange rates in a narrow range, as the Asian countries learned the hard way only recently. Eichengreen, in his prognosis of the future monetary system, goes so far as to say that "it will not be possible to maintain arrangements under which governments commit to preventing exchange rate movements from exceeding explicit limits under all but specific circumstances. . . . Calls for international monetary reform to reestablish a system of pegged but adjustable rates will therefore prove futile." [14]

While finding the flexible exchange rates not totally satisfactory but the fixed rates increasingly unsustainable, some countries are striving for a third way: monetary unification. The European governments were committed to achieving economic and monetary union (EMU) and the introduction of single currency in 1999. In the process, they suffered from an excruciating experience of containing annual budget deficits below 3 percent of GDP. And the reason for this European project is not purely economic, as often assumed. According to Eichengreen, the true motive is one of political economy:

> Exchange rate swings would compound the adjustment difficulties created by the completion of Europe's internal markets. If national industries under pressure from the removal of barriers to intra-European trade find their competitive position eroded further by sudden and "capricious" exchange rate swings, resistance to the creation of the single market would intensity. In this sense and this sense alone, monetary unification is a corollary of factor- and product-market integration.[15]

This same argument applies to the cooperative efforts of the Group of Five (G5) and Group of Seven (G7) in the 1970s and the 1980s. Whenever balance-of-payments problems worsened among the major countries, protectionism reared its head, and in order to put the genie back into the bottle, the G7 governments not only played hardball in trade negotiations but also tried to cooperate in monetary affairs to fend off protectionism. This is what Peter Kenen calls "regime-preserving cooperation." For instance, "the Plaza Communiqué of 1985 . . . was meant to defend the trade regime rather than alter the exchange rate regime."[16] Thus, it is not just the memory of the monetary collapse in the 1930s but the specter of the Smoot-Hawley tariff that impels today's governments and central banks to strive for cooperation.

3.   FRAGILITY OF COOPERATION

Cooperation may seem desirable, but it does not come naturally to strong-willed, sovereign governments and equally independent-minded central banks in the major advanced countries. The most powerful impediment to genuine (as opposed to rhetorical) cooperation is well summarized by Kindleberger's quip, "the buck has no place to stop."[17] Cooperation is a public good, and like a lighthouse, the temptation to free ride is irresistible. This is also known as the collective-action problem.[18] This problem is often presented as the Prisoners' Dilemma game, shown in Figure 1.1, where the numbers in the parentheses are the payoffs (or in this case, ordinal utility) of the two players. The first number in each parenthesis is the payoff of Player A and the second, that of Player B. The players would be relatively satisfied, receiving the second-best payoff of 3 if both cooperated, but as they try to increase their payoff from 3 to 4 by unilaterally defecting, both end up in the suboptimal situation of mutual defection.

		Player B	
		Cooperate	**Defect**
	Cooperate	(3,3)	(1,4)
Player A			
	Defect	(4,1)	(2,2)

Figure 1.1. **Prisoners' Dilemma (PD)**

To take a more concrete (but hypothetical) example, suppose that there is a financial crisis in Korea, and the United States and Japan both benefit if they can relieve the exacerbation of crisis by extending generous credit to the Korean government. But because Japan will still benefit if the United States alone lends the money to calm the panic, Japan has an incentive not to lend or to lend as little as possible, given its domestic troubles. Such behavior may result in too little lending, and the crisis may be prolonged, putting not only Korea but also the United States and Japan in further jeopardy. The suboptimal outcome of the Prisoners' Dilemma plagues many issues in international economic relations because sovereign governments are in principle free to do as they please, and there is nothing to stop them from engaging in socially destructive freeriding.

However, economists have also shown—at least abstractly! —that if this game is repeated again and again, the possibility of cooperation exists even if the players are completely egoistic. The logic is common-sensical. If countries expect to face this kind of situation time and again, they might agree to cooperate each time. Furthermore, they attach a condition: if anyone defects or freerides, other countries will stop helping that country thereafter. If the future is important enough, this threat is credible, and cooperation becomes sustainable for an indefinite period of time.[19] The fact that the importance of future play enables cooperation is known as the "shadow of the future" hypothesis.[20] This hypothesis is useful because it warns us, for instance, that cooperation may be jeopardized when, for reasons such as elections, policymakers become myopic.

4. COOPERATION FAILURES: ABORTED COOPERATION AND COUNTERPRODUCTIVE COOPERATION

Freeriding is an important cause of cooperation, but it is only one aspect of the problem. We can distinguish two categories of cooperation failures: aborted cooperation and counterproductive cooperation.

Aborted cooperation occurs when states attempt cooperation but fail to reach agreement or fail to comply with such agreements for familiar reasons such as freeriding and domestic constraints. In counterproductive cooperation, by contrast, states may cooperate for a while, but they find themselves worse off than before cooperation, and cooperation is therefore suspended in due course.

Students of international relations are familiar with the major reasons for aborted cooperation: freeriding, transaction costs, and domestic constraints. Freeriding occurs because everyone can benefit from the public good provided by someone else's cooperative action; why chip in when you can enjoy international monetary stability anyway? Transaction costs involve necessary negotiation, bargaining, and information costs to be incurred before one reaches a cooperative stage. Even though international institutions are said to lower such transaction costs, they rarely eliminate them,[21] so these costs still continue to present hurdles for successful cooperation. Finally, a variety of domestic constraints—an obstinate legislature, an independent central bank, self-serving and narrow-minded interest groups, and public opinion—may block perfectly public-spirited governments from entering into a cooperative agreement.[22]

	Player B	
	Cooperate	**Defect**
Cooperate	(2,2)	(1,4)
Player A		
Defect	(4,1)	(3,3)

Figure 1.2. **Deadlock**

Counterproductive cooperation is qualitatively different from aborted cooperation, and different causes are involved. It happens, for instance, if the game is something like Figure 1.2, which is known as Deadlock. In this case, the upper-left corner, which is labeled "cooperative," leaves the players worse off than the noncooperative lower-right corner. Game theorists, however, would not usually consider the upper-left corner outcome (Cooperate-Cooperate) as a truly "cooperative" outcome. In this game rational play will lead to mutual defection as in the Prisoners' Dilemma, but it is superior to the nominally cooperative upper-left outcome. It is often argued that international monetary cooperation is counterproductive— meaning that it makes for a worse situation than would occur with a lack of cooperation. Put differently, cooperation can be ineffective and only costly; we must therefore allow for this possibility in our definition of cooperation. Thus, our discussion of cooperation will be based on the following definition:

International cooperation is said to have occurred if sovereign governments or central banks, in light of interdependence of the monetary and financial policies, attempt a deliberate effort to coordinate their policy, reach an explicit (sometimes unwritten) agreement, and act accordingly. In other words, the three essential elements of cooperation are (1) coordination, (2) agreement, and (3) compliance.

According to the definition proposed above, the upper-left corner outcome could be termed "cooperative" even though it is worse than the lower-right "noncooperative" outcome for both players as long as it arose after a process of coordination, agreement, and compliance. Thus, cases such as the upper-left corner of the Deadlock game would count as "counterproductive" cooperation, but is it realistic to think that such a situation will actually occur? Why, that is, would rational players, knowingly agree in the first place? Is not counterproductive cooperation then an oxymoron?

There are several ways to resolve this paradox. First, there may in fact be uncertainty about cooperation. Second, parties that are not involved in the coordination process may affect the outcome. Third, the rationality of players may be compromised due to imperfection in domestic political processes. Fourth, international power play may bring about this paradoxical result. For now let us briefly examine the basic intuition of these four possibilities, which will be developed in greater detail in the next chapter.

First, consider that there is uncertainty about the payoff of cooperation: the payoff of 3 in the upper-left corner in Figure 1.1 may not be certain.[23] Suppose that it could be 4 with a 50 percent chance and 2 with a 50 percent chance: the expected payoff is still 3 as in Figure 1.1. Imagine that the players had a bad draw and that the cooperation payoff was 2 for both players. That means that the game might look like Deadlock *after the fact*, even though cooperation had looked good before they tried it. This in essence is the argument of Jeffrey Frankel, who has demonstrated that there is a considerable amount of scientific uncertainty about the benefits of international monetary cooperation.[24]

Second, the game may involve third parties who are beyond the control of the policymakers who contemplate cooperation. Suppose, for instance, that the cooperation payoff is contingent on the action of these third parties, whether foreign countries or domestic players in the countries of the players. If they act favorably to cooperation, it is beneficial for everyone, but if they react negatively, the cooperation payoff goes down. In that case cooperation may seem counterproductive after the fact. This is the essence of the scenario proposed by Kenneth Rogoff.[25] In his model employment depends on the action of employers and labor unions that set wages on the basis of the expected future course of monetary policy. Monetary authorities in two countries want to boost employment by easing monetary policy without aggravating inflation too much. They may engage in expansionary monetary coordination, but since the labor unions demand high wages in anticipation of this move, real wages do not decline, and employment stays the same as before. Only inflation shoots up as a result. In short, international monetary cooperation is merely inflationary.

A third explanation for paradoxical, counterproductive cooperation is domestic imperfection. In the real world, unlike in abstract theory, there is no guarantee that policymakers will try to maximize the national interest of their country. Policymaking processes may be captured by narrow special interests, in which case international cooperation will be nothing but socially destructive collusion. Such arguments are often made about monetary policy in particular, since the central banks are relatively insulated from normal democratic processes. To the skeptic, whatever central banks do smacks of outright conspiracy. Similarly, it could be argued that monetary policymakers themselves are driven by self-serving interests to the detriment of the economic well-being of society as a whole. Martin Feldstein argues, for example, that policymakers try to divert attention from domestic adjustment by engaging in international cooperation.[26] Cooperation, due to the difficulties generated by freeriding and defection, is bound to fail, and as a result, policymakers neglect necessary domestic adjustments and reform and blame foreigners for the trouble. In circumstances like these, cooperation, or attempts at coordination, can be highly counterproductive.

Finally, counterproductive cooperation may result from international power play. Under their professional cloak, the monetary authorities remain political animals, subject to the temptations of ambition and power play. Suppose that international monetary cooperation occurs in the context of a hybrid game as depicted in Figure 1.3. In this game Player A benefits from cooperation at the expense of Player B. If Player A is powerful and can compel Player B to comply, cooperation (the upper-left corner outcome) will happen, but from B's point of view, it may look counterproductive: the situation is worse than the DD outcome. This is the thesis, in a nutshell, of Stephen Krasner, who argued that international cooperation is nothing but deciding which optimal outcome to choose from a menu of many possible scenarios.[27] Although his argument was made in a slightly different context, the same logic would seem to apply to monetary cooperation as well.

		Player B	
		Cooperate	**Defect**
	Cooperate	(3,2)	(1,4)
Player A			
	Defect	(4,1)	(2,3)

Figure 1.3. **Hybrid of PD and Deadlock**

Each of these four factors is present to some extent in cases of international monetary cooperation, but some may be more important or apparent than others at different times. Thus, one of the most important objectives of this book is to test for these different explanations for counterproductive cooperation. It does not take a degree in economics to hazard a guess, however, that the effectiveness and desirability of international monetary cooperation will probably depend on how it is conducted. There are three main ways in which the advanced industrial countries cooperate in international monetary affairs: (1) collective lending in crises, (2) concerted intervention in the foreign exchange markets and (3) coordination of domestic monetary policy.[28] The last one is the most controversial of all.

The lender-of-last-resort function of the central bank in the domestic economy is the most accepted since Walter Bagehot clarified the problem in the nineteenth century.[29] Since there is no central bank for the international economy as a whole, there is no one responsible for this task should the entire system or a subsystem fall prey to disorder. In today's world, the IMF and the BIS are closest to being international lenders of last resort; but in the face of frequent crises BIS funding is too short-term and the IMF is too slow. The problem of international lending is therefore primarily one of lack or inadequacy and not one of counterproductiveness. Of course, large creditor nations such as the United States and Japan are expected to chip in wherever the stakes involve them, but because of domestic constraints and freeriding, lending is rarely sufficient or decisive enough.

Granted, some aspects of IMF lending have been controversial. Especially, conditionality—attaching a set of conditions such as macroeconomic belt-tightening to its loans—is the target of regular criticism. Because IMF conditionality inflicts enormous financial pain on the masses, borrowing nations invariably detest it. To the extent it helps recover investor confidence, however, it is hard to argue that it is absolutely counterproductive.

The second way in which governments and central banks cooperate in times of crisis, both large and small, is by coordinating foreign exchange intervention. When home currency is in a freefall, the most immediate measure monetary authorities can take is to buy up the currency in the foreign exchange markets. But when the reserves of the central banks are running low, they sometimes ask other central banks to intervene in the markets simultaneously. And doing so in a coordinated manner is sometimes more effective than unilateral action in restoring confidence in the currency. But this type of coordination comes under criticism, in particular, for being is too small to make a difference: when one considers that the gross turnover in foreign exchange markets is more than a trillion dollars a day, official intervention by even the largest central banks on the scale of a few billion dollars a day is merely a drop in a huge ocean. Furthermore, it is also argued that intervention—whether cooperative or not—increases instability in the exchange market. If that were correct, coordinated intervention would be counterproductive.

The third and the most controversial way in which the central banks in the advanced industrial societies collaborate is through coordination of domestic monetary policy. Although monetary policy, such as the targeting of the federal funds rate—the U.S. interbank overnight rate—by the Federal Reserve, is geared primarily at meeting domestic goals, such as keeping inflation and unemployment at sufficiently low levels, it is increasingly subject to international discussion, negotiation, and sometimes coordination—a deliberate change of course. The theoretical case is straightforward: under conditions of high international economic interdependence, one country's monetary policy affects other countries, and to avoid beggar-thy-neighbor policy, it should be placed under international surveillance and if necessary and should be changed to accommodate foreign concerns.[30]

But many argue that such cooperation is counterproductive. From the central bank's point of view, it is dangerous to tie one's own hand in that way, especially in the name of such vague ideas as foreign economic concerns. Second, there is a charge that monetary coordination is too inflationary.[31] Third, to the contrary, the experience of the late 1970s and the late 1980s seems to indicate that international coordination can be too deflationary. Such a danger arises when central banks tie their monetary policy to a country that pursues very tight monetary policy. Fourth, international monetary coordination is often tied to exchange rates, which may not be a good guide for monetary policy. If the primary goal of monetary policy is price stability, which indeed most central banks avow, the exchange rate, even as a policy indicator, makes sense only if imports constitute a significant proportion of domestic consumption. This is not the case with major countries like the United States and Japan, however, where imports are only a small proportion of GDP.

5. SUMMARY

This book begins with the premise that the primary justification for international monetary cooperation is that it is the only hope when the system is in crisis. With or without financial hegemony, cooperation seems to be a prerequisite for a modicum of stability. This is not to say that cooperation is a panacea. All that is claimed here is that the case for international monetary cooperation is strongest when there is an immediate system-wide macroeconomic problem. Except under extreme circumstances each nation should be able to fend for itself.[32]

In this respect, there are three forms of cooperation available to central banks—collaborative crisis lending (collective lenders of last resort), coordination of foreign exchange intervention, and coordination of domestic monetary policy. These cooperative efforts often fail for familiar reasons such as domestic constraints and freeriding. But sometimes, cooperation fails because policymakers find cooperation counterproductive. Why such counterproductiveness happens is less accurately known. Also, the after-effects—and the bitterness—of such experience seem very important and can be long lasting. For instance, monetary cooperation among the G7 governments has significantly declined in the 1990s,[33] and it is likely that this is due to the bitter experience of the 1980s. Thus, it is important to know why such pernicious cases of cooperation could happen in reality.

NOTES

[1] Charles P. Kindleberger, *Mania, Panics, and Crashes: A History of Financial Crises*, 3[d] ed. (New York: Wiley and Sons, 1996).

[2] Charles P. Kindleberger, *The World in Depression, 1929-1939* (Berkeley: University of California Press, 1973): 305. See also Stephen D. Krasner, "State Power and the Structure of International Trade," *World Politics* 28, 3 (April 1976): 317-347; Stephen D. Krasner (ed.) *International Regimes* (Ithaca, NY: Cornell University Press, 1983).

[3] Charles P. Kindleberger, "Dominance and Leadership in the International Economy: Exploitation, Public Goods, and Free Riders," *International Studies Quarterly* 25, 2 (June 1981): 247. See also Kindleberger, *The World in Depression*, 292.

[4] Kindleberger, *The World in Depression*, 299-300.

[5] Kindleberger, *Manias, Panics, and Crashes*, 189.

[6] This is the essence of argument in Robert O. Keohane, *After Hegemony: Cooperation and Discord in the World Political Economy* (Princeton, NJ: Princeton University Press, 1984).

[7] Barry Eichengreen, "Hegemonic Stability Theories of the International Monetary System," in Richard N. Cooper et al., *Can Nations Agree? Issues in International Economic Cooperation* (Washington, D.C.: Brookings Institution, 1989): 255-98.

[8] Ibid., 281. See also Barry Eichengreen, *Golden Fetters: The Gold Standard and the Great Depression, 1919-1939* (New York: Oxford University Press, 1992): 29-66.

[9] Eichengreen, *Golden Fetters*, 11-12.

[10] Eichengreen, "Hegemonic Stability Theories," 287.

[11] Milton Friedman, "The Case for Flexible Exchange Rates," in Milton Friedman, *Essays in Positive Economics* (Chicago: University of Chicago Press, 1953): 175.

[12] *Ibid.*, 173.

[13] Barry Eichengreen, *Globalizing Capital: A History of the International Monetary System* (Princeton: Princeton University Press, 1996): 189.

[14] Barry Eichengreen, *International Monetary Arrangements for the 21st Century* (Washington, D.C.: Brookings Institution, 1994): 4-5.

[15] Barry Eichengreen, "European Monetary Unification," *Journal of Economic Literature* 31 (September 1993): 1322, 1331.

[16] Peter B. Kenen, "The Coordination of Macroeconomic Policies," in William H. Branson, Jacob A. Frenkel, and Morris Goldstein, eds., *International Policy Coordination and Exchange Rate Fluctuations* (Chicago: University of Chicago Press, 1990): 69.

[17] Kindleberger, *The World in Depression,* 300.

[18] Mancur Olson, *The Logic of Collective Action: Public Goods and the Theory of Groups* (Cambridge: Harvard University Press, 1965). Kenneth Oye's explanation of the failure of monetary cooperation in the 1930s and the 1980s relies heavily on this logic. See Oye, *Economic Discrimination and Political Exchange: World Political Economy in the 1930s and 1980s* (Princeton: Princeton University Press, 1992).

[19] The first game-theoretic statement of the possibility of cooperation in repeated PD appeared in James W. Friedman, "A Non-Cooperative Equilibrium for Supergames," *Review of Economic Studies* 38 (1971): 1-12. For an application of this logic to international monetary policy coordination, see Matthew B. Canzoneri and Dale Henderson, *Monetary Policy in Interdependent Economies: A Game-Theoretic Approach* (Cambridge, MA: MIT Press, 1989). Political scientists have used a slightly different framework to arrive at a similar conclusion. If players play tit-for-tat strategies, cooperation could emerge even without ultrarational calculations that are required for the above results. See Robert Axelrod, "The Emergence of Cooperation among Egoists," *American Political Science Review* 75, 2 (June 1981): 306-18 and *The Evolution of Cooperation* (New York: Basic Books, 1984). For an interesting empirical test, see Steve Weber, *Cooperation and Discord in U.S.-Soviet Arms Control* (Princeton: Princeton University Press, 1991).

[20] Kenneth A. Oye, "Cooperation under Anarchy: Hypotheses and Strategies," *World Politics* 38, 1 (October 1985): 1-24.

[21] Robert O. Keohane, "The Demand for International Regimes," *International Organization* 36, 2 (Spring 1982): 141-71; Keohane, *After Hegemony,* 85-109.

[22] See Robert D. Putnam, "Diplomacy and Domestic Politics: The Logic of Two-Level Games," *International Organization* 42, 3 (Summer 1988): 427-60. Putnam's work generated a research program that led to a number of theory-guided empirical research projects in the 1990s. For representative work, see Peter B. Evans, Harold K. Jacobson, and Robert D. Putnam, eds, *Double-Edged Diplomacy: International Bargaining and Domestic Politics* (Berkeley: University of California Press, 1993): 171-206; Kyoji Fukao and Koichi Hamada, "International Tariff Negotiations and Domestic Economic Conflicts: A Common Agency Approach," unpublished paper (January 1992); Koichi Hamada, "International Negotiations and Domestic Conflicts: A Case for Counter-Lobbying," Lawrence R. Klein ed., *A Quest for a More Stable World Economic System: Restructuring at a Time of Cyclical Adjustment* (Dordecht and Norwell, MA: Kluwer Academic, 1993): 23-40; Keisuke Iida, "When and How Do Domestic Constraints Matter? Two-Level Games with Uncertainty," *Journal of Conflict Resolution* 37, 3 (September 1993): 403-426; Keisuke Iida, "Involuntary Defection in Two-Level Games," *Public Choice* 89, 3-4 (December 1996): 283-303; Howard P. Lehman and Jennifer L. McCoy, "The Dynamics of the Two-Level Bargaining Game," *World Politics* 44, 4 (July 1992): 600-644; Helen V. Milner, *Interests, Institutions, and Information: Domestic Politics and International Relations* (Princeton, NJ: Princeton University Press, 1997); Helen V. Milner and B. Peter Rosendorff, "Trade Negotiations, Information and Domestic Politics: The Role of

Domestic Groups," *Economics and Politics* 8, 2 (July 1996): 145-89; Jongryn Mo, "The Logic of Two-Level Games with Endogenous Domestic Coalitions," *Journal of Conflict Resolution* 38, 3 (September 1994): 402-422; Jongryn Mo, "Domestic Institutions and International Bargaining: The Role of Agent Veto in Two-Level Games," *American Political Science Review* 89, 4 (December 1995): 914-24; Leonard J. Schoppa, "Two-Level Games and Bargaining Outcomes: Why Gaiatsu Succeeds in Japan in Some Cases but Not Others," *International Organization* 47, 3 (Summer 1993): 353-86; Leonard J. Schoppa, *Bargaining with Japan: What American Pressure Can Do and Cannot Do* (New York: Columbia University Press, 1997); Domestic politics is also important in terms of determining who adjusts how. See C. Randall, Henning, *Currencies and Politics in the United States, Germany, and Japan* (Washington, D.C.: Institute for International Economics, 1994); Yoshiko Kojo, *Keizaiteki Sogoizon to Kokka: Kokusai Shushi Fukinko Zesei no Seiji Keizaigaku* (Economic Interdependence and the State: The Political Economy of International Balance-of-Payments Adjustments) (Tokyo: Bokutakusha, 1996); Yoshiko Kojo, "Economic Internationalization, Domestic Preferences, and Policy Choices: U.S.-Japan Payments Imbalance Adjustment Since the 1970s," Paper prepared for delivery at the 1997 Annual Meeting of the American Political Science Association, Sheraton Washington and the Omini Shoreham, August 28-31, 1997; Beth A. Simmons, *Who Adjusts?: Domestic Sources of Foreign Economic Policy during the Interwar Years* (Princeton, NJ: Princeton University Press, 1994); Beth A. Simmons, "Rulers of the Game: Central Bank Independence During the Interwar Years," *International Organization* 50, 3 (Summer 1996): 407-43.

[23] Now we are taking the payoffs to be cardinal utility instead of ordinal utility.

[24] Jeffrey A. Frankel, *Obstacles to International Macroeconomic Policy Coordination*, Princeton Studies in International Finance, 64 (Princeton: International Finance Section, Department of Economics, Princeton University, 1988).

[25] Kenneth Rogoff, "Can International Monetary Policy Cooperation Be Counterproductive?" *Journal of International Economics*, 18, 3-4 (May 1995): 199-217.

[26] Martin Feldstein, "Thinking about International Economic Coordination," *Journal of Economic Perspectives* 2, 2 (Spring 1988): 1-13.

[27] Stephen D. Krasner, "Global Communications and National Power: Life on the Pareto Frontier," *World Politics* 43, 3 (April 1991): 336-66.

[28] There are other ways in which nations cooperate in international finance, such as cooperation in supervision and regulation of banking and in taxation of multinational corporations. These regulatory cooperation cases are outside the scope of this book for a variety of reasons. Some cooperation episodes are microeconomic, such as cooperation to go after international rogue banks such as BCCI. Although these may be important for the world financial order, they are qualitatively different from the macroeconomic cooperation studied in this book. Second, some of these financial cooperation episodes such as the establishment of international financial institutions are meant to prevent crises or solve long-term problems rather than the short- to medium-term problems of a macroeconomic nature addressed in this book. Again these are hard to compare. Third, regulatory cooperation is more sporadic, and there are not enough cases to test for alternative explanations.

[29] Walter Bagehot, *Lombard Street: A Description of the Money Market* (London: C. Kegan Paul, 1878).

[30] Koichi Hamada, "A Strategic Analysis of Monetary Interdependence," *Journal of Political Economy* 84, 4 (August 1976): 677-700; *The Political Economy of International Monetary Interdependence* (Cambridge, Mass.: MIT Press, 1985).

[31] See Rogoff, "Can International Monetary Policy Cooperation Be Counterproductive?"

[32] For a very strong argument to this effect, see Karl Otto Pöhl, "You Can't Robotize Policymaking," *International Economy* 1, 1 (October/November 1987): 20-26.

[33] See C. Fred Bergsten and C. Randall Henning, *Global Economic Leadership and the Group of Seven* (Washington, D.C.: Institute for International Economics, 1996).

Chapter 2

Theories of Counterproductive Cooperation

1. INTRODUCTION

We have seen that there are two kinds of cooperation failures: aborted cooperation and counterproductive cooperation. Aborted cooperation refers to attempts at cooperation that do not yield expected results, because some of the essential elements of cooperation—coordination, agreement, and compliance—do not materialize for such familiar reasons as freeriding, domestic constraints, and transaction costs. These instances of cooperation failures are well understood and will not be pursued here. Counterproductive cooperation, by contrast, is less well studied and less understood: we seek to study why it occurs and what its consequences are.

Reading the literature closely, however, one finds that there is already a variety of theories and arguments about counterproductive cooperation, but they are not fully developed or synthesized. These theories can be divided roughly into four broad categories, although they exhibit some overlap.

The first class of theories focuses on third-party effects. When there are third parties whose behavior is consequential, cooperation can become counterproductive. The second class of theories suggests that policymakers may have some perverse, noneconomic goals or biases that may be exacerbated by cooperation. The third group highlights uncertainty involved in international cooperation. When policymakers have incomplete knowledge about how the international monetary system works or how to conduct monetary policy properly to attain their economic goals, cooperation can fail to produce desired results. Finally, the last set of theories looks at the exercise of power at the international level, for example, such as coercion and signaling. Coercion is a demand on foreign partners to accede to one's plans with an explicit or implicit threat of punishment. Signaling is a costly action to demonstrate one's resolve about a particular course of action. Although theoretically distinct, coercion and signaling are empirically indistinguishable in many cases; it therefore seems appropriate to consider them together.

2.   THIRD PARTY EFFECTS

When there are third parties who are excluded from cooperation but who can affect the outcome in a material way, there is no guarantee that cooperation will yield beneficial results. The excluded parties may react or preempt the cooperative deal in a negative way to the detriment of the cooperating parties.

In political economy, the most important "third" parties are markets: The conflict or lack of coordination between governments and markets is a common theme. Indeed, the essence of the rational expectations revolution in macroeconomics was the proposition that market expectations about official policy may render policy ineffective or produce results that are not anticipated by policymakers. Policymakers' incentives change over time, for example, even if they plan rationally at the beginning. Unless policymakers can credibly commit themselves to their original plans, markets will expect a change of course later on and hence yield the outcomes that are radically different from the original plan. This time-inconsistency theorem popularized by Kydland and Prescott has been applied to many different areas of macroeconomics.[1]

One of the most celebrated applications of this theory to monetary policy is the so-called Barro-Gordon model.[2] Barro and Gordon assume that the expectational Phillips curve describes the trade-off between employment and inflation: market participants have expectations as to the future rate of inflation, and it is only when the actual rate of inflation deviates significantly from the expected rate of inflation that the Phillips curve trade-off comes into play. In other words, if the actual rate of inflation exceeds the expected rate of inflation, real wages will go down because nominal wage contracts are based on expected rates of inflation, and reduced real wages will increase employment. Conversely, as long as the expected rate of inflation matches the actual rate, inflation does not affect the real economy; it is as if there were zero inflation except that all parties must adjust their price tags, nominal interest rates, nominal wage rates, and so on, by the expected rate of inflation.

Now, if this expectational Phillips curve is in operation, the Keynesian prescription for reducing unemployment and boosting economic growth becomes much more treacherous than under the traditional Phillips curve analysis. Suppose we start with zero inflation and the natural rate of unemployment. What if the government, for one reason or another, decides to reduce unemployment below the natural rate? It can increase the rate of money supply growth and produce surprise inflation. But as market participants begin to anticipate it, they will adjust their inflationary expectations upward, and the expectational Phillips curve moves upward, incorporating the higher expected rate of inflation. The government may try to reduce unemployment again by surprising the public, but then the expected rate of inflation will ratchet up again, and so on. This process will continue until inflation is so bad that the government has no more incentive to reduce unemployment because of the risk of fueling further inflationary pressures. Over the long run, then, the government cannot reduce unemployment below the natural rate. The Barro-Gordon model goes a step further. It assumes that the government has an incentive to surprise the public but that market participants are well aware of this and will therefore anticipate a high rate of inflation from the outset. Thus, according to this theory, discretionary monetary policy is highly inflationary while having no effect on the real economy (unemployment or output).

Kenneth Rogoff has applied this theory to the international coordination of monetary policy.[3] Like Barro and Gordon, he assumes that the government has an incentive to reduce unemployment and boost economic growth by increasing the money supply at a faster rate than the public anticipates. Without coordination, the currency of the government that is trying to ease monetary policy will depreciate rapidly; if the government cares about exchange rate stability, the fear of currency depreciation will deter the government from experimenting with this inflationary measure. But if the governments of two interdependent economies have this motive simultaneously, they could coordinate their monetary easing together, thereby avoiding the risk of currency depreciation. But again, rational market agents will anticipate such coordination and adjust their expectations upward beforehand, nullifying the effects of monetary easing on the real economy. In this way, international monetary policy coordination, like discretionary monetary policy in the Barro-Gordon closed-economy model, could be inflationary while producing no real benefits. If correct, it is a very strong indictment of monetary policy coordination.

Not only is this an elegant theory whose conclusions are striking but it also seems to fit some stylized facts about G7 policy coordination in the 1970s and 1980s: the Bonn summit agreement of 1978, in which Japan and Germany promised to expand their economies, was closely followed by the second oil crisis and worldwide inflation; the Louvre Accord of 1987, in which Japan and Germany promised some expansionary policies, was followed by financial bubbles in Japan, which continued even after Black Monday in October which witnessed worldwide stock crashes. In light of these experiences, the Japanese and Germans have sworn not to repeat the same mistakes by mortgaging their monetary policies to the vagaries of G7 cooperation. Does this mean that the theory of counterproductive policy coordination is a valid explanation for failures in G7 policy coordination? We will pursue this question in Chapter 3.

The Rogoff model, in which market expectations undermine the intended reflationary effects of monetary cooperation, is one illustration of a larger point: any third parties, who do not necessarily have to be market agents, can render international cooperation problematical. For instance, Canzoneri and Henderson constructed a three-economy model where two countries cooperate while excluding the third. In that model, cooperation can lower the welfare of the countries involved in coordination as well as that of the excluded party. They state that "it is worth observing that this result [regarding counterproductive exclusionary cooperation] is not really so paradoxical. It is well known that in games with three or more players, if some players form a coalition of the type we have considered, one or more members of the coalition may end up worse off than if each player acts individually."[4]

Another key point embedded in the Rogoff model is that policymakers try to lower unemployment to a level below the natural rate. Like Barro and Gordon, Rogoff assumes that this comes from a benign motive, such as offsetting the effects of distortionary taxation. But the same motive may come from different, sometimes more pernicious sources, and in real life, it is hard to distinguish between them. In other words, the Rogoff model is also related to our second set of theories, which focuses on some perverse, noneconomic motives of policymakers. Such perverse incentive could lead to bad policy, and cooperation, by removing constraints on bad policy, may make the situation even worse.

3.   PERVERSE INCENTIVES

There are models that emphasize a government's noneconomic motives for pursuing policies that may not be desirable from society's point of view. Furthermore, if two or more governments share those pernicious incentives, international cooperation aggravates these biases. In this instance, international cooperation can be highly counterproductive and undesirable.

Guido Tabellini proposes a model of fiscal policy coordination that closely resembles the Rogoff model.[5] In his model, two major parties compete for office. Once in office, the winning party runs fiscal policy, including deciding how much government debt to take on. The parties have different preferences about the composition of public goods to consume in each period. The voters' preferences are distributed in such a way that neither party is elected with certainty. Another country, which trades with the first country, has the same structure of politics and economics. Tabellini shows (1) that balanced budgets are ex ante (namely, before governments are chosen) optimal from international society's point of view, (2) that if left to pursue discretionary policy, governments in both countries will pursue budget deficits, and (3) that if they coordinate fiscal policies, budget deficits are larger than policies pursued unilaterally and hence farther away from optimal zero deficits. This model has close parallels to the Rogoff model, but there are some differences. First, the perversity of the government's incentives arises from partisanship and elections. Since they are not certain that they will be reelected, they will try to consume more of their favorite public goods than if they knew for certain that they would be in office in the future. In other words, the costs of debt are not fully internalized by the partisan governments. Thus, the incentives are more misaligned than in the Rogoff model. Susanne Lohmann has constructed a similar though more complex model, in which two highly partisan parties conduct monetary policy. She shows that partisan electoral cycles (policy changes according to partisanship after elections) can be exacerbated by coordination.[6] The reasons for this counterproductive volatility in policy arise from the same political incentives: partisanship and elections.

As opposed to these deductive models, which are based on sophisticated economic models and abstraction, Martin Feldstein, a former chairman of the Council of Economic Advisers (CEA), argued on the basis of his observation of actual G7 cooperation that international monetary cooperation is highly counterproductive. In a series of articles and speeches, he criticized international monetary coordination as practiced in the late 1980s for four reasons.[7] First, he argues that the G7's practice of targeting *nominal* exchange rates is not appropriate since external balances depend on real, not nominal, exchange rates. Second, he argues that model uncertainty in international economics is such that the costs could easily outweigh the benefits of policy coordination no matter how good its intention may be: "When there are fundamental disagreements about the way the world economy works, there is little reason to believe that coordinated policy will produce improved performance."[8] Third, he argues that the constitutional separation of powers in the United States precludes international coordination of American fiscal policy; as a result, the burden of adjustment is placed on monetary policy, leading to misguided policy coordination. Fourth and finally, he opposes international policy coordination because it distracts policymakers from necessary policy adjustments at home:

> An emphasis on international interdependence instead of sound domestic policies makes foreign governments the natural scapegoats for any poor economic performance. Pressing a foreign government to alter its domestic economic policies is itself a source of friction and the making of unkeepable promises can only lead to resentment.[9]

An example he had in mind was the budget deficit problem in the United States. It was clear to most people that large U.S. current account deficits of the 1980s largely stemmed from the equally large budget deficits in the United States. Instead of tackling the latter problem head on, however, the U.S. government tried to depreciate the dollar and to force foreign economies to make adjustments. In particular, the U.S. government pressured Japan and Germany to increase their domestic demand by easy money and expansionary fiscal policy. Japan eventually complied, but Germany obstinately refused to ease monetary policy.

Thus, Treasury Secretary Baker accused Germany of reneging on cooperation in the fall of 1987, when German monetary policy was tightened. Some felt that this U.S.-German row was partly responsible for the stock market crash in October. The United States and its partners would have been much better off, had they not entered into international monetary cooperation. In brief, the syndrome of bashing foreigners for domestic economic ills is often a concomitant of international policy coordination. This indictment of international monetary coordination is different from the Barro-Gordon-Rogoff model or the Tabellini-Lohmann models. Based on his insightful reflection on the actual practice of G7 policy coordination in the 1980s, Feldstein is the more convincing.

The third and fourth points he makes belong to this section, because the essence of counterproductiveness lies in perverse political incentives: incentives of fiscal authorities to shift the burden of adjustment to monetary policy, even if the latter may not be the appropriate instrument, and incentives of politicians to blame foreigners for economic ills that in fact may be homegrown. International cooperation (or foreigners' refusal to cooperate) may provide a perfect excuse for politicians looking to escape electoral punishment for the economic problems that they invented in the first place.

4. UNCERTAINTY

Alternatively, cooperation can be counterproductive in the face of imprecise knowledge of the world economy. Just as one is unlikely to reach his or her destination using an unreliable or outdated road map, policy may backfire if it follows a misguided blueprint. Although this is a problem that can arise with any policy, it is particularly acute in international monetary cooperation because of fundamental disagreements among different nations about how the economy works, and what kind of policy is suited to tackle contemporary problems. Jeffrey Frankel contributed enormously to clarifying this problem.

First, he pointed out that there are significant differences among various econometric models of the world economy used by government economists to make their economic forecasts.[10] For instance, one model may predict that the U.S. economy will expand by 1 percent a year if U.S. fiscal policy is expanded by a half percent of GDP, while another model may predict it will grow by an additional 2 percent. This kind of difference will naturally influence economists' assessment of the net benefits of international macroeconomic policy coordination. To take a simple example, suppose that the United States and Japan simultaneously expanded their fiscal policy by 1 percent of their GDP. Model A predicts that this will increase economic growth by 2 percent and increase inflation by 1 percent in both countries. This may seem like a beneficial outcome. On the other hand, suppose that Model B predicts that economic growth increases by only 1 percent but inflation will increase by 3 percent in both countries. It is unlikely that the governments will find cooperation worthwhile in this instance. Thus, the expected benefits and costs of cooperation hinge on which model the governments use to forecast the outcome.

Next, Frankel and Rockett conducted a series of computer simulations using some prominent macroeconomic models, generating a thousand model combinations.[11] Out of the thousand possible combinations of models, policy coordination turned out to be counterproductive for the United States in 286 cases and for Europe in 298 cases, according to the assumed true model. This is because models that are different from the true model could prescribe excessive tightening or easing. Thus, they conclude: "the danger that coordination will worsen welfare rather than improve it is more than just a pathological counterexample."[12]

While highly intuitive and persuasive, this theory has been subjected to some criticisms. Holtham and Hughes Hallet argue, for instance, that if international cooperation requires both governments to expect joint gains according to their respective beliefs, the incidence of counterproductive coordination should be lower than that suggested by Frankel and Rockett.[13] Ghosh and Masson assert that as governments learn about the true model, coordination is more likely to benefit the participating countries than to hurt them.[14]

While these criticisms of the theory of model uncertainty are valid to some extent, their arguments are not very convincing in view of the actual practice of G7 cooperation. First, the Group of Seven, although all major industrial countries, is not a group of equals. The U.S. economy is still a dominant influence because of its sheer size and concomitant political clout. Accordingly, the U.S. view often prevails even in the face of opposition from other countries. Therefore, as long as the U.S. government thinks that coordination can be useful, the G7 countries may coordinate their policies. This pattern was observed in both the 1970s and the 1980s: the locomotive theory was essentially an American idea that was tried despite Japanese and German opposition; coordinated easing of monetary policy in 1986-87 was also mainly an American idea, although there were also some sympathizers in Japan. Thus, if the American model is flawed, it can easily result in misguided policy cooperation.

The learning argument, while valid in the abstract, does not fully eliminate the problem of model uncertainty in practice. As Ghosh and Masson admit, the macroeconomy is a "noisy" system with an enormous amount of disturbances and extraneous factors. Therefore, revision of macroeconomic models to improve forecasts and policy prescription is a very slow process that evolves over the course of years. The problem is further compounded by cognitive rigidity. Unlike quantitative macroeconomic models, which economists revise according to new data and statistical laws, models that are relevant at the policy level in monetary and fiscal policy-making are highly subjective, leaving a much larger role to human judgment, which is often resistant to change.

Another possibility that model uncertainty may cause "seemingly" counterproductive cooperation is suggested by Ghosh and Masson, who show that the cooperative outcome, if uncertainty is fully taken into account, is still beneficial ex ante. But then how can cooperation be counterproductive? The answer may be that given the uncertainty, the ex post result may seem counterproductive to the third-party observers who do not take the ex ante uncertainty into account. In that sense, counterproductiveness is a result of actual uncertainty as well as the lack of observers' failure to take note of it. Suppose that I made investments after a careful assessment of risks involved and that my investments go sour. My wife may accuse me of reckless investments and lack of business acumen after the fact. Similarly, it is always easy for critics to accuse policymakers of errors after the fact. But given the uncertainty, the policymakers may have chosen an ex ante optimal course of action.[15]

5. COERCION AND SIGNALING

After each incidence of economic policy coordination in the 1970s and the 1980s, the Germans and Japanese complained bitterly about the fruitlessness and even counterproductiveness of cooperation. This suggests that they may have been coerced into cooperation, rather than cooperating voluntarily.

Chancellor Helmut Schmidt, for example, one of the engineers of the Bonn summit agreement, since has become a tough critic of international monetary cooperation among the major industrial countries. He describes the typical process as follows:

> The locomotive theory [on which the Bonn agreement was based] has since grown into a monster of the Loch Ness type: It keeps coming up for air. The first optimistic call for a new beginning is invariably followed by a second call to change course, and the other nations are asked to help *while their national economic interests are ignored.* The third act then consists of dramatically aggravated conflicts of interest. These cannot be genuinely resolved in the fourth and final act but are more or less swept under the rug with mere declarations of intention.[16]

This statement is not a direct testament to coercion, but certainly it hints at it.

Academics tend to be more candid about the existence of coercion in U.S.-Japan and U.S.-German macroeconomic relations. Randall Henning talks of a "dollar weapon" used by the United States to bulldoze Japan and Germany into cooperating:

> When the United States conflicts with other countries over the proper level of world aggregate demand, or the distribution of demand among the Group of Five (G-5) countries, for example, macroeconomic and declaratory policies promoting dollar depreciation provide incentives to foreign governments to conform with American wishes. . . . [T]he United States is not invulnerable to adverse effects of dollar depreciation or appreciation on its own rates of inflation and growth. But, because it has a large and, arguably, relatively autonomous economy, the United States is less susceptible to these effects than are its economic partners. That asymmetry is fundamental.[17]

Signaling is yet another power concept that is similar but theoretically distinct from coercion. In international relations, signaling is often associated with showing one's resolve or commitment. Thomas Schelling suggested various ways in which states could demonstrate their resolve by engaging in nuclear brinkmanship.[18] Students of economic sanctions, too, have suggested that sanctions are not simply an instrument of coercion (to inflict costs on the target) but are sometimes also an instrument of signaling (which inflicts costs on the sender).[19] As economic sanctions inflict costs on both sender and target, coercion and signaling become empirically hard to distinguish. The dollar weapon also suffers from the same problem: it inflicts costs on both the United States and the target state—usually Japan or Germany. But either way in practical terms, it is a means for the United States to push Japan or Germany to comply with American wishes.

The only difference, if any, between coercion and signaling is the degree of intended malice. The point of coercion is to inflict or to threaten to inflict significant costs on the target. The target state will naturally be enormously resentful. By contrast, the point of signaling is to communicate some intangible message to the target—the costs inflicted on the target are therefore only incidental. Thus, even though the target will not like it, the perception of malice will be much less severe, and consequently the damage to the diplomatic relationship between the two countries will be smaller.

But here is the rub. Since the same act can be interpreted either as a signal or as a coercive act, the target can easily misinterpret the true intention. Thus, even if the American government insisted that its economic sanctions were only a signal of its resolve and had no coercive intent, the message could fall on deaf ears.

6.   METHODOLOGICAL CONUNDRUM

All of these theories are persuasive to some extent. Unfortunately, however, none has been subjected to systematic empirical tests, and therefore, we do not have very strong confidence as to whether any of these theories has any relevance for the actual practice of cooperation. This deplorable state of knowledge needs to be improved on.

Testing these models with any empirical materials, however, raises some intractable methodological problems. Foremost is the uncertainty about what the objective function (economists' jargon for the national economic interest) of the country should be or what the objective function of policymakers should look like. While economists largely agree that employment (and/or real growth of the economy), inflation, and current account deficits (if need be) should be part of the objective functions, but the question is how much weight should be given to each. Ranking these different objectives generates deep disagreements between economists and policymakers. Thus, to come up with a national "average" of these different preferences is no mean task. What usually happens in real life is that these different preferences of policymakers (who represent some segments of the population) are aggregated in a somewhat arbitrary way, with the preferences of the leaders in power assigned the greatest weight.[20] Whether such aggregation correctly reflects the true average national preferences is anybody's guess. Furthermore, there is a theoretical argument that to attain a desirable macroeconomic outcome, monetary policymakers should be more inflation-hawkish than the average person in the economy.[21] Again, it is not clear whether the real-life decision-making mechanism is designed to reflect this bias.

One possible way out of this conundrum is to estimate what the objective function (if any) looks like if we assume the government as a whole is trying to maximize such a function. In one of the few attempts at such estimation, Oudiz and Sachs concluded that the U.S. government seems to put almost zero weight on current account deficits as a goal.[22] This finding should be taken with a grain of salt. The estimation is sensitive to several factors. First, it uses data from the first term of the Reagan administration, which indeed was heavily inward looking in its conduct of macroeconomic policy-making. But it is doubtful that the preferences of the Reagan administration are reflective of the nation as a whole or of American government in general. The Oudiz-Sachs finding is also baffling because many episodes of cooperation among the major industrial countries are specifically aimed at reducing current account imbalances. Thus, if we accept the assumption that the U.S. government cares little about these imbalances, it is not surprising that Oudiz and Sachs concluded that coordination was not particularly beneficial. The only point made here is that Oudiz-Sachs study, though otherwise very valuable, is a reminder that estimation of official objective functions is very problematical.

In terms of the purpose of this book, uncertainty about the objective function is a serious problem because counterproductiveness of monetary cooperation is highly sensitive to the specification of the objective functions. Take a very simple example. Suppose that there are two policy targets, say, unemployment and inflation, and the policymaker's objective function is to minimize a weighted average of these two indicators. Unless the cooperation outcome dominates the uncooperative outcome (that is, both inflation and unemployment are lower under cooperation), cooperation can be deemed counterproductive from some policymaker's point of view. For instance, suppose that unemployment and inflation rates are 6 percent and 2 percent, respectively, under noncooperation and that they are 4 percent and 4 percent under cooperation. For a policymaker who tries to minimize a simple arithmetic average of these two targets, these outcomes are equivalent (the misery index = 8 in both outcomes), but for any policymaker who puts a weight heavier than ½ on inflation, the cooperative outcome is worse than the noncooperative outcome. Because there is no unambiguous right answer about how much weight to assign these targets, these judgments become highly problematical.

There are two more empirical problems. First, a lack of counterfactuals: when cooperation actually takes place, we do not know what would have happened without it. Depending on what we expect would have happened, cooperation could be deemed a success or a failure. For instance, if we assume that without monetary cooperation there would have been a major trade war and a breakdown of the world trading system, it could be considered a success. But of course we do not know whether such catastrophes would in fact have occurred. A second difficulty is that of endogeneity. It is easy enough for critics to demonstrate that monetary cooperation is counterproductive because it increases external imbalances. Indeed, each episode of G3 cooperation is highly correlated with large current account deficits in the United States (See Figure 2.1). But that is not a consequence of G3 cooperation but the very motive behind it. Other economic indicators may suffer from the same problem.

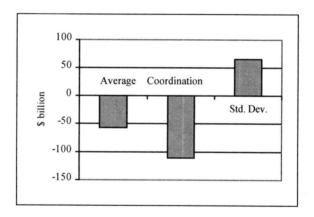

Figure 2.1. **U.S. current account balances
in average and coordination years**
Source: *International Financial Statistics,* 1970-96

For these reasons, conducting a simple test of the theories of counterproductive cooperation is a difficult matter. This book seeks to circumvent these problems in two ways. The first is simply to assume that some aspects of these models are valid to some extent and to see if further deductions from the theory correspond to the data. Thus, for instance, the Rogoff model assumes that the monetary policymakers target only unemployment and inflation and nothing else (such as current account deficits). Furthermore, the model assumes that policy does not have long-term effects on either monetary or real outcomes. If one is willing to accept these assumptions, it is then legitimate to ask if inflation is actually higher under coordination than under noncoordination (see Chapter 3). The second method is to assume the theory of model uncertainty is correct and to use policymakers' behavior as an indicator of counterproductiveness. If policymakers find cooperation to be counterproductive, given their policy objectives, they will reduce cooperation over time. In a world of perfect information, if policymakers knew for sure that cooperation were counterproductive, this kind of learning would not take place, but given the uncertainty involved, it is natural to assume that some learning occurs in reality. If, however, policymakers learn that cooperation is beneficial overall, they will continue or increase the frequency and intensity of cooperation. But such learning can be detected in the highly detailed data, and because of the data limitations, this method is applied to foreign exchange intervention data alone.[23]

7. SUMMARY

This chapter has reviewed four major explanations or classes of models of counterproductive cooperation. The first, represented by the Rogoff model, focuses on third-party effects, especially those of the markets. If the markets automatically raise their inflationary expectations at the first sign of international monetary cooperation, policymakers may be forced into cooperation just to avoid recession. The second model, which overlaps somewhat with the first, focuses on the perverse incentives that arise from noneconomic, often political, mechanisms and institutions (such as elections). If policymakers have such pernicious incentives, there is no guarantee that cooperation will better the economic interests of the nations involved. In such a scenario, cooperation is more accurately termed collusion.

The third model, represented by Frankel's theory underlines uncertainty as the source of counterproductiveness. The intuition is a powerful one: if policymakers do not know what they are doing, it is unlikely that cooperation will improve the situation.

Finally, political scientists focus on power exercises such as coercion and signaling as a possible source of counterproductive cooperation. Even though cooperation may promote the interest of the coercer/signal-sender in terms of material outcomes, the overall result may be worse than noncooperation if one takes into account the costs of coercion (risks that costly punishment has to be imposed in the case of non-compliance) and signaling (costly behavior to demonstrate resolve).

Testing for any of these theories is a daunting task for empirical researchers, the greatest obstacle being that we have no good knowledge of what the national economic interest should be or what the policymaker's objective function looks like. Since empirically estimating policymakers' objective functions is fraught with difficulties, one needs to circumvent the problem when testing for the above theories of counterproductive cooperation. This book proposes and executes two different methods, as well as plausibility probes by case studies.

APPENDIX

This appendix proposes a model of seemingly counterproductive cooperation: the cooperative solution in the model is optimal ex ante, but after the realization of a shock, it can be deemed inferior to the noncooperative equilibrium. We use the Canzoneri-Henderson two-symmetric-country economy with a productivity shock, which the central banks try to accommodate. We assume furthermore that the central banks pursue only price objectives. In this case, without model uncertainty, the Nash equilibrium and international cooperative solutions are the same. In the presence of model uncertainty, however, international cooperation is likely to be more efficient than noncooperation according to Ghosh and Masson.[24] Canzoneri and Henderson show that with symmetric productivity shocks, prices in the two countries can be represented as follows:

$$q = m + \theta(m - m^e) - \rho(m^* - m^{*e}) + x,$$

$$q^* = m^* + \theta(m^* - m^{*e}) - \rho(m - m^e) + x,$$

where m is the logarithm of the money supply, q is the logarithm of the consumer price index, x is a symmetric productivity shock, which is an i.i.d. random variable with mean zero and variance σ^2_x, the variables with asterisks are foreign variables, and the superscript e denotes the expectation operator.[25]

The loss functions of the central banks include only price objectives:

$$L = E(q^2),$$

$$L^* = E(q^{*2}).$$

Since market expectations are formed before the realization of shocks and the central banks decide the money supply after observing the actual shock, expectations cannot completely match the actual money supply in the model. It can be readily checked that both Nash and cooperative outcomes are the same:

$$m^N = m^{*N} = m^C = m^{*C} = -x/(1 + \theta - \rho),$$

where the superscript N denotes the Nash equilibrium and the superscript C denotes cooperation. This is simply a special case of the well-established result that if each country pursues a single policy objective, each can maximize its gains unilaterally.

Now we introduce model uncertainty. Let θ and ρ be i.i.d. random variables, θ with mean μ_θ and variance σ^2_θ and ρ with mean μ_ρ and variance σ^2_ρ. These random variables and the productivity shock are assumed to be independent. Policy is decided without observing the realized values of θ and ρ. In this case, the Nash equilibrium and the cooperative outcome typically differ as long as $\mu_\rho \neq 0$ and $\sigma^2_\rho \neq 0$:

$$m^N = m^{*N} = -x(1+\mu_\theta)/[(1+\mu_\theta)(1+\mu_\theta-\mu_\rho)+\sigma^2_\theta],$$

$$m^C = m^{*C} = -x(1+\mu_\theta-\mu_\rho)/[(1+\mu_\theta-\mu_\rho)^2+\sigma^2_\theta+\sigma^2_\rho].$$

Furthermore,

$$L^N = L^{*N} = \sigma^2_x[(\sigma^2_\theta+\sigma^2_\rho)B^2+\sigma^4_\theta]/(AB+\sigma^2_\theta)^2,$$

$$L^C = L^{*C} = \sigma^2_x(\sigma^2_\theta+\sigma^2_\rho)/(A^2+\sigma^2_\theta+\sigma^2_\rho),$$

where $A=1+\mu_\theta-\mu_\rho$ and $B=1+\mu_\theta$.

It can be checked that $L^N > L^C$, and hence that cooperation is more efficient ex ante than noncooperation. This replicates the Ghosh and Masson result.[26]

How is this result to be reconciled with the argument that model uncertainty can make international cooperation counterproductive? It turns out that the above efficiency result applies to only ex ante expectations: ex post, however, cooperation may not be better than noncooperation. Suppose, for example, that $\sigma^2_\theta=0$ and that σ^2_ρ is large. Furthermore, suppose that the realized value of ρ is close to its mean value but that the realization of x has turned out to be a large positive value. Both countries will try to offset this inflationary shock by tightening monetary policy, but the cooperative solution does not offset it completely whereas the Nash equilibrium does. Thus, it appears ex post as if cooperation were worse than noncooperation. But this does not contradict the ex ante efficiency result.

NOTES

[1] See, for instance, the papers included in Torsten Persson and Guido Tabellini, eds., *Monetary and Fiscal Policy, Vol. 1: Credibility* (Cambridge, Mass.: MIT Press, 1994).

[2] Robert J. Barro and David B. Gordon, "A Positive Theory of Monetary Policy in a Natural Rate Model," *Journal of Political Economy* 91, 4 (August 1983): 589-610; idem, "Rules, Discretion and Reputation in a Model of Monetary Policy," *Journal of Monetary Economics* 12, 1 (July 1983): 101-21. For a critical review, see Keith Blackburn and Michael Christensen, "Monetary Policy and Policy Credibility: Theories and Evidence," *Journal of Economic Literature* 27, 1 (March 1989): 1-45. This theory has generated many related literatures in Political Economy. Especially relevant to the study of monetary policy are the literature on central bank independence and another on central bank secrecy. For the former, see Alex Cukierman, *Central Bank Strategy, Credibility and Independence* (Cambridge, Mass.: MIT Press, 1992); Alex Cukierman, Steven B. Webb, and Bilin Neyapti, "Measuring the Independence of Central Banks and Its Effects on Policy Outcomes," *World Bank Economic Review* 6, 3 (September 1992): 353-98; John B. Goodman, *Monetary Sovereignty: The Politics of Central Banking in Western Europe*

(Ithaca, N.Y.: Cornell University Press, 1992); John T. Woolley, *Monetary Politics: The Federal Reserve and the Politics of Monetary Policy* (Cambridge: Cambridge University Press, 1984). For the latter, see Richard Cothren, "Asymmetric Information, Optimal Money Growth Targets, and Fed Secrecy in a Monetary Policy Game," *Journal of Macroeconomics* 12, 4 (Fall 1990): 599-609; Alex Cukierman and Allan H. Meltzer, "A Theory of Ambiguity, Credibility, and Inflation Under Discretion and Asymmetric Information," *Econometrica* 54, 5 (September 1986): 1099-1128; Marvin Goodfriend, "Monetary Mystique: Secrecy and Central Banking, *Journal of Monetary Economics* 17, 1 (January 1986): 63-92; Karen K. Lewis, "Why Doesn't Society Minimize Central Bank Secrecy?," *Economic Inquiry* 29, 3 (July 1991): 403-15; Jeremy R. Rudin, "Central Bank Secrecy, 'Fed Watching', and the Predictability of Interest Rates," *Journal of Monetary Economics* 22, 2 (September 1988): 317-34; Jeremy C. Stein, "Cheap Talk and the Fed: A Theory of Imprecise Policy Announcements," *American Economic Review* 79, 1 (March 1989): 32-42; Guido Tabellini, "Domestic Politics and the International Coordination of Fiscal Policies," *Journal of International Economics* 28, 3-4 (May 1990): 245-65.

[3] Kenneth Rogoff, "Can International Monetary Policy Cooperation Be Counterproductive?" *Journal of International Economics* 18, 3-4 (May 1985): 199-217.

[4] Matthew B. Canzoneri and Dale W. Henderson, *Monetary Policy in Interdependent Economies: A Game-Theoretic Approach* (Cambridge: MIT Press, 1991): 73.

[5] Guido Tabellini, "Domestic Politics and the International Coordination of Fiscal Policies," *Journal of International Economics* 28, 3-4 (May 1990): 245-65.

[6] Susanne Lohmann, "Electoral Cycles and International Policy Cooperation." *European Economic Review* 37, 7 (October 1993): 1373-91.

[7] Martin Feldstein, "Correcting the Trade Deficit," *Foreign Affairs* 65, 2 (Spring 1987): 795-806; idem, "Thinking about International Economic Coordination," *Journal of Economic Perspectives* 2, 2 (Spring 1988): 3-13; Feldstein, ed. *International Economic Cooperation* (Chicago: University of Chicago Press, 1988); idem, "The Case Against Trying to Stabilize the Dollar," *American Economic Review* 79, 2 (May 1989): 36-40.

[8] Feldstein, "Thinking about International Economic Coordination," 11.

[9] Ibid., 12.

[10] Jeffrey A. Frankel, *Obstacles to International Macroeconomic Policy Coordination*, Princeton Studies in International Finance 64 (Princeton: International Finance Section, Department of Economics, Princeton University, December 1988).

[11] Jeffrey A. Frankel and Katherine E. Rockett, "International Macroeconomic Policy Coordination When Policymakers Do Not Agree on the True Model," *American Economic Review* 78, 3 (June 1988): 318-40.

[12] Ibid., 330.

[13] Gerald Holtham and Andrew Hughes Hallett, "International Policy Cooperation and Model Uncertainty," in Ralph Bryant and Richard Portes, eds., *Global Macroeconomics: Policy Conflict and Cooperation* (Houndmills, Hampshire: Macmillan, 1987): 128-77, see especially, 160-62.

[14] Atish R.Ghosh and Paul R. Masson, "International Policy Coordination in a World with Model Uncertainty," *IMF Staff Papers* 35, 2 (June 1988): 230-58; idem, "Model Uncertainty, Learning, and the Gains from Coordination," *American Economic Review* 81, 3 (June 1991): 465-79.

[15] See the appendix to this chapter for a formal exposition.

[16] Helmut Schmidt, *Men and Powers: A Political Retrospective*, trans. Ruth Hein (New York: Random House, 1989): 266-67; emphasis added.

[17] C. Randall Henning, Macroeconomic *Diplomacy in the 1980s: Domestic Politics and International Conflict among the United States, Japan, and Europe*, Atlantic Paper 65 (London: Croom Helm, 1987): 3-4.

[18] Thomas C. Schelling, *Arms and Influence* (New Haven: Yale University Press, 1966), chaps. 2-3.

[19] David A. Baldwin, *Economic Statecraft* (Princeton: Princeton University Press, 1985); Lisa L. Martin, *Coercive Cooperation: Explaining Multilateral Economic Sanctions* (Princeton: Princeton University Press, 1992).

[20] For instance, Chappell, Havrilesky, and McGregor estimate whose preferences are heavily weighted in the decisions made by the Federal Reserve and find that the preferences of the chairman of the Federal Reserve Board weigh heavily. See Henry W. Chappell, Jr., Thomas M. Havrilesky, and Rob Roy McGregor, "Partisan Monetary Policy: Presidential Influence through the Power of Appointment," *Quarterly Journal of Economics* 108, 1 (February 1993): 185-218; idem, "Monetary Preferences of Individual FOMC Members: A Content Analysis of the Memoranda of Discussion." *Journal of Economics and Statistics* 79, 3 (August 1997): 454-60.

[21] See Kenneth Rogoff, "The Optimal Degrees of Commitment to an Intermediate Monetary Target," *Quarterly Journal of Economics* 100, 4 (November 1985): 1169-90.

[22] This result is accorindg to the MCM model but not according to the EPA model. See Gilles Oudiz and Jeffrey Sachs, "Macroeconomic Policy Coordination among the Industrial Economies," *Brookings Papers on Economic Activity* 1 (1984): Table 9, 40. Indeed, they argue that "the advent of the Reagan administration and the much smaller weight it placed on the current account deficit probably reduced the attractiveness of policy coordination for the United States." Oudiz and Sachs, 44.

[23] This test is reported in the appendix to Chapter 4.

[24] Atish R. Ghosh and Paul R. Masson, *Economic Cooperation in an Uncertain World* (Cambridge: Blackwell, 1994).

[25] Matthew B. Canzoneri and Dale W. Henderson, *Monetary Policy in Interdependent Economies: A Game-Theoretic Approach* (Cambridge: MIT Press, 1991): 14.

[26] Ghosh and Masson, *Economic Cooperation in an Uncertain World*, 61.

Chapter 3

Counterproductive Monetary Policy Coordination

1. INTRODUCTION

This chapter considers the theory of counterproductive cooperation by examining the actual cases of coordination of macroeconomic policies among the major industrial countries during the 1970s and 1980s. It begins with a bird's-eye view of some of empirical evidence relevant to the four theories developed in the previous chapter; the evidence is all consistent with the theories. The chapter then presents two case studies, both of which are presumed by at least some observers to have been counterproductive.

In doing this exercise, we find that while there is some evidence to show that all the explanations have some validity, only one is consistently supported: the theory of model uncertainty. In both case studies, there were enough uncertainties about the effects of proposed cooperation. And both cases could be interpreted as counterproductive at least according to some of the models. Thus, it is not surprising that both cases are still controversial.

The appendix to this chapter analyzes the data on the political economy of U.S.-Japan monetary relations more closely. Direct tests of the theories using this data set are difficult to execute, as discussed in the previous chapter. But we can nevertheless detect some patterns in the data that show whether they are consistent with the behavioral implications of the different models.

2.   OVERVIEW

There is a strong view, held mainly in Germany, that international monetary
policy coordination is inflationary.[1] And there is some evidence that this may
be true. Figures 3.1, 3.2, and 3.3 show the growth rates of the money supply
in the United States, Germany, and Japan. The left-most bar in each shows
the average annual growth rate of M1 in the United States, that of M3 in
Germany and that of M2+CD in Japan from 1973 (the first year of the float)
to 1996. The center bar in each figure is the average growth of these money
supply indicators in each country in 1978 and 1986-87 when monetary
policy coordination occurred. All show that in coordination years money
supply growth was faster than average; in Germany, however, the difference
is less clear.

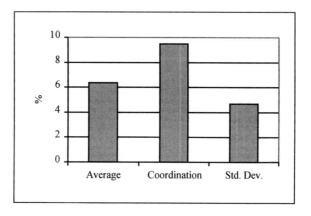

Figure 3.1. **Growth of M1 in the United States
in average and coordination years**
Source: *International Financial Statistics* (IMF); Period 1973-96.

For the Rogoff model to be empirically valid, inflation has to be higher
than without cooperation and unemployment must not be significantly
different from noncooperation. This is hard to test because inflation and
unemployment are also affected by other factors. Another difficulty is
uncertainty about the lag of policy effects. It may take some time for given
policy to be reflected in economic outcomes, and cooperation is no
exception to this rule. Given this uncertainty, Figures 3.4, 3.5, and 3.6 use
different combinations of years to see the effects of coordination.

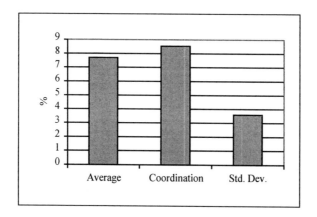

Figure 3.2. **Growth of M3 in Germany**
in average and coordination years
Source: *International Financial Statistics* (IMF); Period 1973-96

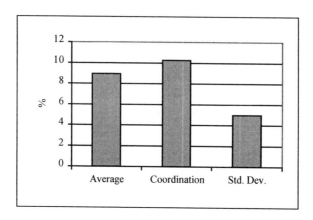

Figure 3.3. **Growth of M2+CD in Japan**
in average and coordination years
Source: *Economic Statistics of Japan* (Bank of Japan); Period 1973-96.

These figures compare the average inflation rate, the average unemployment and the average value of the misery index (the sum of inflation and unemployment) for each of the three countries from 1975 to 1997 (1978-1996 in Germany) on the left-most side of the graph. These averages are compared with the average of the same rates for four combinations of coordination (or after-effect) years. The bars termed Coordination #1 show these averages for 1978 and 1986-1987 only (that is, no lag effects are considered). Coordination #2 includes these coordination years and one year afterward (1978-79, 1986-88). Coordination #3 shows

only the one-year lag effect after each coordination (1979, 1987-88) Finally
Coordination #4 includes the effects of both a one-year-lag and a two-year
lag (1979-80, 1987-89). The standard deviation of each variable is also
displayed on the right-most part of the graph. None of the coordination
averages are notably higher than the series averages, but the inflation rate
and the misery index are somewhat higher than the series averages in the
United States, if one allows for two-year-lag effects. This is consistent with
the Rogoff model. But overall, there does not seem to be strong evidence of
counterproductiveness in these macroeconomic statistics.

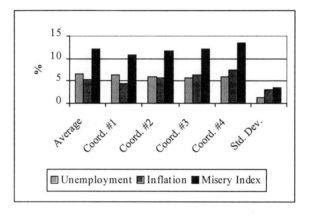

Figure 3.4. **U.S. misery index in average and coordination years**
Source: Datastream; Period 1975-97

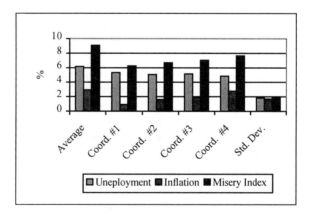

Figure 3.5. **German misery index in average and coordination years**
Source: Datastream; Period 1978-96

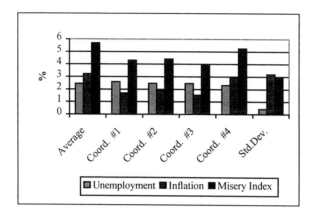

Figure 3.6. **Japanese misery index in average and coordination years**
Source: Datastream; Period 1975-97

The Tabellini model can be tested similarly by examining whether the budget deficits are larger in coordination years than otherwise. Figures 3.7 through 3.9 show the government deficits as percentages of GDP in each of the three countries. The left-most bar is the average for the period from 1973 to 1996, the center bar is the average for the two years when fiscal policy was putatively coordinated (1978 and 1987), and the right-most bar is the standard deviation for the series. Only in Japan is the proportion of deficits to GDP higher than average. This could be interpreted in two different ways: either that coordination takes effect only on Japanese policy or that fiscal policy was coordinated in all of the countries but was conducted in such a way that deficits were not significantly larger than without coordination.[2] Only the second interpretation is contrary to the Tabellini model.

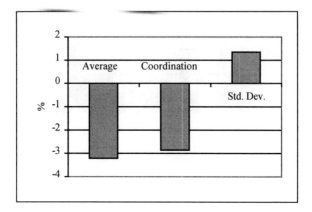

Figure 3.7. **U.S. budget balance as percentage of GDP
in average and coordination years**
Source: *International Financial Statistics* (IMF); Period 1973-96

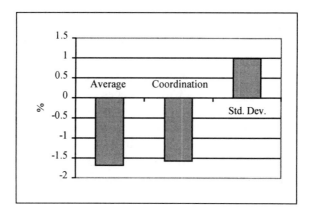

Figure 3.8. **German budget balance as percentage of GDP
in average and coordination years**
Source: *International Financial Statistics* (IMF); Period 1973-96

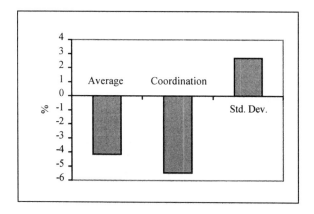

Figure 3.9. **Japanese budget balance as percentage of GDP
in average and coordination years**
Source: *International Financial Statistics* (IMF); Period 1973-96

Overall, aside from money supply data, the statistical evidence is not particularly clear on the validity of the Rogoff and Tabellini models.

The model uncertainty theory à la Frankel is hard to demonstrate statistically. Table 3.1 gives some sense of disagreement among different models that are often used. The values shown are various estimates of the policy multipliers (for instance, the multipliers of U.S. monetary policy on U.S. output, and so on). The index in the right column (ς) shows the degree of consistency among the different models: the higher this index, the higher the degree of agreement among the models.

Table 3.1. **Uncertainty in parameter estimates in 12 macroeconomic models**

	Mean μ	Variance σ^2	$\varsigma = \mu^2/(\sigma^2+\mu^2)$
U.S. on U.S. output	0.288	0.034	0.71
U.S. on U.S. inflation	0.218	0.060	0.44
U.S. on ROW output	-0.085	0.009	0.45
U.S. on ROW inflation	-0.010	0.009	0.012
ROW on ROW output	0.159	0.009	0.72
ROW on ROW inflation	0.134	0.054	0.25
ROW on US inflation	-0.134	0.055	0.24
ROW on US output	0.068	0.019	0.019

Source: Atish R. Ghosh and Paul R. Masson, *Economic Cooperation in an Uncertain World* (Oxford: Blackwell, 1994), Table 2-1, p. 29.

Not surprisingly, this index takes very low values on international multipliers, such as the effect of U.S. monetary policy on the rest of the world (ROW). This is certainly consistent with Frankel's theory. The only weakness of this kind of exercise is that there is no guarantee that policymakers actually rely on these econometric models in making policy. Rather, policymakers tend to use no small dose of discretion and political judgment in deciding monetary policy. Thus, this table is not a direct confirmation that policymakers will actually disagree in the face of uncertainty.

Finally, Figures 3.10 through 3.12 show the degree of pressure exerted by the United States on Japanese macroeconomic policy. This is a coding of the number of articles that appeared in a major Japanese financial newspaper, *Nihon Keizai Shimbun*, regarding U.S. political pressures on Japanese macroeconomic policy.[3] Figure 3.10 shows the number of articles mentioning U.S. pressure on Japan to cut interest rates. There is no evidence for American pressure for raising interest rates; this simple fact is consistent with the Rogoff model mentioned above. There are two periods of concentrated U.S. pressure on Japan: 1986-87 and 1991. The pressures in 1986-87 did result in substantial easing of Japanese monetary policy as detailed below, whereas the pressure in 1991 produced no tangible results.[4] Figure 3.11 shows the incidence of U.S. pressure on Japanese measures to boost domestic demand, usually implying loosening fiscal policy. The period 1986-87 was characterized by systematic exertion of pressure on this front as before. And there are two other periods of intense pressures: 1977-78 (see the case of the Bonn summit below) and 1993 (the first year of the Clinton administration). As shown below, the pressures in 1977-78 yielded some fiscal measures, but the pressure was fended off in 1993. Figure 3.12 combines the two and shows that three periods—1977-78, 1986-87, and 1991-93— saw intense U.S. pressure on Japan.

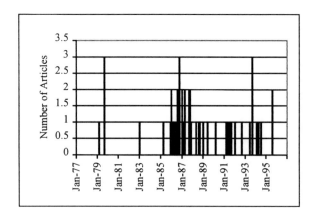

Figure 3.10. **U.S. pressure on Japan to cut interest rates**
Source: *Nihon Keizai Shimbun*

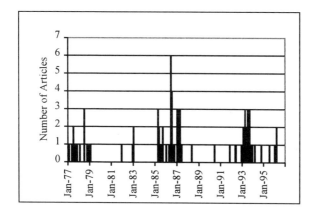

Figure 3.11. **U.S. pressure on Japan to expand domestic demand**
Source: *Nihon Keizai Shimbun*

It should be noted, however, that this is not a strict test of the coercion hypothesis per se, for two reasons. First, pressures reflected in these newspaper articles are only indirectly connected with coercion and only some of the time; a stick may accompany soft words or harsh words are accompanied by no threat of retaliation for noncompliance. Second, coordination may not be always counterproductive, even from the point of view of the target of pressure. To test for the coercion hypothesis directly, one needs a direct measure of coercion and a direct measure of perception of counterproductiveness.

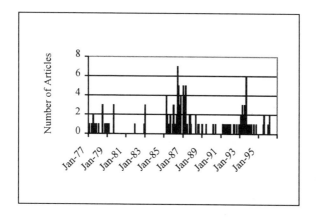

Figure 3.12. **Total U.S. pressure on Japan**
Source: *Nihon Keizai Shimbun*

As a consequence, the test reported in the appendix is also only an indirect test for the coercion hypothesis. The difficulty of measuring the perception of counterproductiveness is perhaps the greater challenge for the empirical tests of the theory. Only in two cases of coordination can we find sufficient evidence for such perception: the Bonn summit of 1978 and the Louvre Accord of 1987. Therefore, the remainder of this chapter concentrates on these two alleged cases of counterproductive coordination.

3.   CASE NO. 1: THE BONN SUMMIT AGREEMENT

The first case is the story of the locomotive theory that the Carter administration initiated in 1977, leading to the well-known agreement at the Bonn economic summit meeting in July 1978. The American initiative met with staunch German and Japanese resistance at first, but eventually agreement was reached with Japan in late 1977, and then with Germany at the summit itself. The agreement was implemented, but the second oil crisis hit later in the year, and the primary problem turned from sluggish growth to worldwide inflation. Thus, the Bonn agreement quickly became obsolete. Although the American participants welcomed the agreement, the Germans and Japanese widely perceived it as a major policy failure.   From the German and Japanese perspectives, the Bonn summit agreement looked like a case of counterproductive cooperation. So why did this happen?[5]

The locomotive theory, a rationale for coordination, was invented in 1976, when some of the major industrial countries were still staggering from the impact of the first oil shock of 1973/74. The quadrupling of oil prices due to the oil embargo by the Organization of Petroleum Exporting Countries (OPEC) on the occasion of the Yom Kipper War had a major worldwide impact, with inflation quickly followed by recession in 1974 and 1975. Also, all the net oil importers suffered from current account deficits. Only the three major industrial countries—the United States, Japan, and Germany—recovered quickly from the external deficits and recession. By contrast, the other industrial countries in Europe, particularly Britain, France, and Italy, continued to reel from the shock, triggering projectionist pressures.

Against this background, economists in the so-called trilateral countries—the members of the Trilateral Commission—proposed that the United States, Japan, and Germany expand their economies to assist the other countries in their economic recovery. For instance, sixteen economists who gathered at the Brookings Institution, a major liberal think tank in Washington, called on the governments of the three countries to take reflationary policies to relieve the burden of deficits in Europe and oil-importing developing countries.[6] Economists at the Organization for Economic Cooperation and Development (OECD) in Paris called for a similar action.

President-elect Carter chose such enthusiastic trilaterists for the top economic policy posts. The new administration was also under pressure from both labor unions and business groups to undertake an expansionary fiscal policy, but unilateral expansion could be risky under conditions of increasing international interdependence. One of the economic advisers says that immediately before the inauguration, there was a consensus among his top economic policymakers on two points: (1) that the recovery from the 1975 recession was faltering and some additional stimulus was necessary, and (2) that if the United States alone provided the stimulus, it would result in undesirable downward pressure on the dollar, which would fuel inflationary expectations.[7]

Although this Keynesian argument had some resonance in Germany, the German government had serious doubts about the soundness of this economic scenario. The result was a series of confrontations between Germany and the United States in 1977-78. When Vice President Walter Mondale visited Germany soon after the inauguration, the United States issued an ultimatum. In essence,

> [t]he Americans served notice on Bonn that their domestic program would be implemented regardless of what the chancellor chose to do. The Americans predicted that if he chose not to stimulate the German economy, the American current account deficit and the German surplus would grow, with predictable effects on the foreign exchange markets. Were the German government to continue its restrictive course, it should be prepared to countenance the domestic ramifications of substantial appreciation of the deutsche mark relative to the dollar.[8]

German Chancellor Helmut Schmidt rebutted the American proposal by arguing that additional fiscal stimulus would not have expansionary effects on the economy and that faster German growth would not have a strong impact on partner countries.[9] Similarly, at an OECD meeting in the spring of 1977, the German delegate argued that Keynesian measures aimed at fine-tuning and boosting the economy would no longer work. Because people's belief in the stability of money had been destroyed, he said, traditional pump-priming methods of raising the government deficit were no longer effective.[10] Although Schmidt was somewhat sympathetic to Keynesianism, he expressed similar doubts: "I am not convinced that the vulgar Keynesian economics, which some politicians have now adopted 30 years after Keynes, is really the way to judge a much more complicated situation." He assessed the current situation "not just a downward business cycle but a deep structural crisis, to which Keynesianism was not a solution."[11]

As for the possible damage from the unilateral expansion threatened by the United States, the Germans appeared to agree. By observing the growing U.S. deficits during the first months of the Carter administration, Hans Apel, German finance minister, warned against underestimating the serious dangers of monetary instability that could result from high and continuous U.S. current account deficits.[12]

	Germany	
	Expansion	**No expansion**
U.S.		
Expansion	High growth Moderate inflation	Moderate growth Dollar depreciation U.S. deficits
No expansion	---	Low growth Low inflation

Figure 3.13. **U.S. view of policy coordination, 1977-78**

	Germany	
	Expansion	**No expansion**
U.S.		
Expansion	No additional growth High inflation	Dollar depreciation U.S. deficits
No expansion	---	Low growth Low inflation

Figure 3.14. **German view of policy coordination, 1977-78**

Figures 3.13 and 3.14 summarize the U.S. and German views at that time. The most striking difference was that the United States predicted higher growth than did Germany (for both countries as well as for their trading partners). As a result, the U.S. government perceived joint expansion to be much more desirable than Germany did. But both the Carter administration and the German government agreed on one point that unilateral U.S. expansion would be undesirable for the United States because of current account deficits and for Germany because of dollar depreciation.

The United States made similar demands on the Japanese government led by a new prime minister, Takeo Fukuda. The Japanese reaction to the U.S. request was somewhat different from that of Germany, however. At a meeting with Vice President Mondale Fukuda is reported to have expressed understanding of Japan's locomotive role and stressed his commitment to the growth and current-account targets.[13] This was in line with his established policy goal of attaining 6.7 percent real growth in the Japanese fiscal year 1977. Economists, however, had been privately expressing doubt that government policy was aggressive enough to reach the target. Despite the calls for more audacious fiscal and monetary policy from within the ruling Liberal Democratic Party (LDP), the Ministry of Finance continued to hold the ceiling for the bond financing of budget deficits to 30 percent of the budget. In light of these constraints in Germany and Japan, it is no surprise that the London summit in May 1977 endorsed only those growth goals that had been announced by individual governments well before the meeting.

In the face of German resistance and Japanese timidity, the United States embarked on a course of unilateral expansion. The Carter administration's fiscal policy was more expansionary than his predecessor's had been. Although the administration capitulated to Congressional opposition and abandoned a $50-per-capita tax rebate plan, most other fiscal policy programs passed Congress, providing an additional stimulus of $32.3 billion. Monetary policy, although restrained by the independent-minded Federal Reserve, was also looser than in the previous years. During 1977, M1 grew by 7.9 percent. In terms of economic outcomes, the growth benefit of stimulus certainly appeared: U.S. real GNP grew by 5.3 percent during 1977. However, the cost of expansion was inflation and current account deficits. The GNP deflator, an indicator of inflation, grew by 6 percent, and the current account deficit increased to a postwar record of $18.5 billion. During 1977, the dollar also depreciated by 10.8 percent against the mark and by 22.3 percent against the yen.[14]

U.S. policymakers were well aware that their action in the absence of German and Japanese expansion was costly to the United States; U.S. officials repeatedly stressed the costs of the unilateral expansion at international meetings. In mid-1977 the U.S. delegate to the OECD warned that if Germany and Japan did not expand their economies faster, the United States would face a dangerous balance-of-payments deficit that might arouse calls for protectionism at home and monetary turmoil abroad. Another U.S. official said, "The fact is that we are bleeding when others are not."[15]

Unilateral U.S. expansion was also perceived as costly to Germany. Although Germany had been aiming at 5 percent real growth in 1977, growth faltered toward the end of that year, resulting in a paltry 2.6 percent figure. While there were many causes of this sluggish growth, some of which were purely domestic, most German observers agreed that rapid appreciation of the mark against the dollar—perceived as a consequence of U.S. expansion—was depressing investment. As early as in the summer of 1977, Finance Minister Apel complained that the abruptness of the mark's rise against the dollar had upset German businessmen and delivered a "shock to our economy."[16] The mark's appreciation and slower-than-expected growth in Germany had a predictable effect—an increasing number of people and institutions began to demand fiscal stimulus as a cure for the economy. In the autumn of 1977 the fiscally conservative Bundesbank cited the deflationary effect of deutsche mark appreciation as an additional reason why an expansionary package would be acceptable.[17]

In the meantime, Japan also was feeling the effect of the sharp appreciation of the yen, which had begun in the fall: it moved from a high of 266 yen to the dollar on September 29 to 240 yen by November 24. The Bank of Japan intervened in the market, furiously trying to peg the rate to 240 yen per dollar.[18] The U.S. subcabinet-level mission to Tokyo in September demanded unspecified economic stimuli. Henry Owen, a White House consultant and President Carter's summit "sherpa," came up with an idea of a specific growth target for JFY 1978 of about 7-8 percent.[19] For its part, the Japanese bureaucracy was unanimous in the view that anything beyond 6 percent growth was a pipe dream. By a political sleight of hand, a compromise target of 7 percent emerged in December.[20]

And as the new year was ushered in, change of attitude was also emerging in Germany. Hans Matthöfer, who replaced Hans Apel as finance minister at the beginning of 1978, was much more audacious in fiscal policy-making. In May he rejected "rigid formulae" in the area of public spending and said that he felt that pump-priming must depend on the current economic situation.[21] Soon afterward he directed the Ministry of Technology to come up with bold spending programs.

As German attitudes toward the locomotive theory softened, agreement at the upcoming summit meeting in Bonn became more likely. Chancellor Schmidt was reluctant to make a unilateral concession, however; instead, he insisted that the United States correct its energy policy, which had kept U.S. oil prices artificially low in comparison with the world standard. Finally, on the second day of the July summit meeting, the German government made a concession by promising to expand its fiscal policy by the 1 percent of GNP that the Carter administration had been demanding. As a quid pro quo the

American government promised to raise U.S. oil prices to world levels by 1980.

The bargain at the Bonn summit was implemented without defection: the German government introduced a package of public spending and tax cuts, totaling DM 12.25 billion. In the following spring the Carter administration announced that the United States would gradually lift price controls on domestic crude oil.[22] Japan, however, failed to attain the 7 percent growth target despite the supplemental budget introduced in the summer of 1978.

The post-summit evaluation of the agreement is highly asymmetrical. U.S. participants tend to be sanguine about the experience. For instance, Anthony Solomon, undersecretary of the Treasury at that time, recalled that "the [Bonn summit] agreement was sound in principle and was a significant contribution" and that "the potential benefits from the package as a whole appeared to far outweigh any of the potential costs."[23]

But the German and Japanese participants and observers, by contrast, are invariably negative in their assessment of the episode. Helmut Schmidt, one of the protagonists, has since been a harsh critic of the Bonn agreement. Similarly, officials from the Japanese Ministry of Finance (MOF) have been almost unanimous in their criticism. A former MOF official underscores their negative evaluation:

> The essential mistake at Bonn, and at all those exercises throughout the years, was an obsession with a fine-tuning approach. The United States thought it was feasible to set up certain quantitative goals and target our macroeconomic performance. It was a *fundamental mistake*, for example, for Japan to accept such a precise target as growth of 6.7 percent.[24]

4. EVALUATION OF ALTERNATIVE THEORIES

We see, then, that there is some evidence that the Germans and Japanese considered the Bonn summit agreement counterproductive for themselves certainly and for the rest of the world, because of the burst of inflation, the dollar crisis of 1978, and the legacy of budget deficits.

In looking for the cause of this seemingly counterproductive cooperation, we find that all of the major theories fit the story to some extent, so the episode cannot be a decisive test for comparing alternative theories. Nevertheless, one can arrive at some judgments about how useful each perspective is for understanding this and other possible cases of counterproductive cooperation.

4.1. The Rogoff Model

The Rogoff model is attractive in the sense that it perfectly fits the fact that the Bonn summit agreement was followed by the burst of inflation later in the year. And this was at least partly due to expansion of monetary policy.

Despite the resemblance to the model, however, there are some weaknesses as well. First, the locomotive theory did not specify monetary policy as an instrument. The United States was explicit about fiscal expansion in Germany. The U.S. demand on Japan was unclear about which instrument to use, but for obvious reasons, politicians focused on fiscal policy. Although the Ministry of Finance had some influence over monetary policy, it is controlled by the Bank of Japan (at least on paper). Second, the second oil shock was as much to blame for worldwide inflation as this episode of joint reflation. Inflation from 1979 onwards was, for example, the result of "imported inflation." Thus, after careful analysis, Holtham concluded that "the contribution of the post-Bonn measures to inflation was certainly small and probably negligible."[25]

Of course, another interpretation, offered by Ronald McKinnon, is that global inflation, including the second oil shock, was due to an abrupt increase in the world money supply in the late 1970s.[26] It would be fair to say that monetary policy was eased in both Germany and Japan in 1978 partly because of their concerns about the effects of exchange rate appreciation on their competitiveness and about its recessionary impact. But this thesis is still controversial.[27] And there seems no academic consensus whether the world money supply is a valid concept.

4.2. The Tabellini Model

To the extent that the Bonn episode of cooperation focused on fiscal policy, the Tabellini model, which predicts a budget deficit bias in fiscal policy coordination, may offer the better explanation. There is much talk about the deficit legacy of the Bonn agreement. For instance, the Japanese budget deficit reached a historic high of 6.1 percent of GNP in 1979, after which the Ministry of Finance decided to embark on a program of fiscal austerity. But Table 3.2 fails to convince us that this was solely due to international coordination. Rather, the trend toward an increasing gap had started long before the Bonn agreement. And the source of this shortfall seems predominantly domestic: expansion of the welfare state without a corresponding increase in tax revenues. If anything, international commitment only had the effect of delaying the MOF's effort of fiscal austerity.

Table 3.2. **Japanese budget deficits in the 1970s**

Fiscal year	General account deficits (billion yen)	Ratio of deficits to GNP (percent)
1971	1,187	1.5
1972	1,950	2.1
1973	1,766	1.6
1974	2,160	1.6
1975	5,281	3.6
1976	7,198	4.3
1977	9,561	5.2
1978	10,674	5.2
1979	13,472	6.1
1980	14,170	5.9

Source: Edward J. Lincoln, *Japan: Facing Economic Maturity* (Washington, D.C.: Brookings, 1988): 93.

A similar point can be made about Germany as well. Although net government borrowing increased from 2.5 percent of GNP in 1978 to 2.7 percent in 1979, reaching a high of 4 percent in 1981, this trend had started in the early 1970s. Moreover, the high figure in 1981 is the result of recession, which was a consequence of lack of coordination after 1978.

Overall, that fiscal policy coordination expanded budget deficits in all of the locomotive countries accords with the Tabellini model, but it is hard to ascribe solely to the Bonn summit agreement.

4.3. Model Uncertainty

We saw that the Germans were quite skeptical about the locomotive theory. Asked if he believed in the locomotive theory, Matthöfer replied: "Nobody thought that Carter was an economist. The idea was for Germany to pull the world economy from the recession, and it is ridicuous. Our trade with the United States is only a small percentage of our trade, and foreign trade is only a small part of the GNP."[28] He rued that "it was not thought out by economists."

More specifically, the German government had learned since the breakdown of the Bretton Woods system that fiscal policy no longer affected the real economy as it once had under the fixed exchange rate regime. The German government had adjusted fiscal policy time and again before the Bonn agreement, but to no effect. And since Republican administrations in the United States had not practiced fiscal fine-tuning since 1973, this lesson was lost on the new Carter administration. Thus this asymmetry in perception was clearly due to model uncertainty and to disagreement about the transmission effects, as Frankel pointed out.

As a result, the German government refused to go along with the locomotive theory, resulting in a lopsided pattern of expansion in 1977. This led to the turmoil in exchange markets, which finally convinced the Germans and Japanese that the lack of cooperation was worse than (possibly counterproductive) cooperation.

4.4. Coercion

Given the uncertainty that the Germans and to some extent the Japanese felt about the validity of the locomotive theory, it is no surprise that it was also perceived to be counterproductive even in retrospect. Then why did they agree? It is after all the right of sovereign states to refuse any cooperative agreement they think is unwise.

This question naturally suggests the possibility that the Germans and Japanese were coerced into the agreement, whether explicitly or implicitly. And there was the usual suspect—talking down the dollar: in 1977 Treasury Secretary Michael Blumenthal was repeatedly suspected of being guilty of doing just that. The Japanese media, with its fondness for calling these external events "shocks" (such as the oil "shocks" and Nixon "shocks"), dubbed these events "Blumenthal shocks." The research into whether or not Blumenthal's careless remarks were deliberate attempts to influence the markets or even to coerce the Japanese and Germans into compliance has generated mixed conclusions. For instance, after sorting through evidence, Cohen and Meltzer conclude that "[t]ruth would appear to lie between the two extremes of malevolence (i.e., coercion) and total innocence."[29]

Regardless, however, there is no denying that the Japanese and Germans were strongly alarmed by American exchange rate policy during 1977. Testifying before the Budget Committee of the Diet a day after the so-called second Blumenthal shock, Bank of Japan Governor Teiichiro Morinaga expressed his discomfort: "There is evidence that speculation was triggered by Treasury Secretary Blumenthal's 'unwitting remark' that yen appreciation has not been enough." [30] Similar negative reactions could be heard in Germany at this time.

Furthermore, the Japanese compliance with reflation was partly a function of their perception that yen appreciation was hurting their exports and that an expansion of domestic demand to offset the decline in exports was necessary. In that sense, the U.S. coercion strategy, whether intended or not, worked like a magic. But at what costs?

5. CASE NO.2: THE LOUVRE ACCORD

The Louvre Accord of February 22, 1987, and subsequent loosening of Japanese monetary policy is suspected of triggering the bubble economy of the late 1980s in Japan. Thus, this case is considered a prime example of counterproductive monetary cooperation.

The genesis of the policy coordination episode dates back to the first term of the Reagan administration, which practiced so-called Reaganomics. Under the influence of the supply-siders such as David Stockman, the Reagan administration sought to trim the federal government by implementing large tax and spending cuts. It did cut taxes, but not spending. Budget deficits soared as a result, and the current account deficits increased in tandem. This twin deficit problem was the motive of the subsequent cooperation efforts among the G5 and G7 nations. First, the G5 finance ministers and central bank governors tried to correct the U.S. current account deficits by devaluing the dollar through coordinated intervention in an agreement made at the Plaza Hotel in New York on September 22, 1985. This episode will be analyzed in the next chapter.

After finding this measure inadequate, the G5 and G7 nations shifted to coordinating fiscal and monetary policy. The adjustment of fiscal policy would have made more sense; on balance, U.S. fiscal policy was too loose in this period, and German and Japanese fiscal policies were a little too tight. But U.S. fiscal policy was hard to change due to the political gridlock in Congress, and the fiscal authorities in Japan and Germany resisted fiscal adjustments as well. Thus, the burden of adjustment was diverted to monetary policy in these countries. In 1986-87 the U.S. administration persistently pressured Japan and Germany to ease monetary policy, ostensibly to boost their domestic demand. The Japanese readily complied because they were worried about the speed with which the yen was appreciating after the Plaza agreement. The culmination of this monetary policy coordination was the Louvre Accord, when the Japanese interest rate was cut to a historic low. The Germans were less compliant, and as soon as inflationary pressures were detected, the Bundesbank switched to tightening. By the G7 meeting in Berlin in September 1988, the group's top priority had shifted to fighting inflation. But Japan lagged behind in this change. The Bank of Japan was still under the spell of the international commitment to exchange rate stability since the Louvre Accord, while unchecked speculation in real estate and stock markets triggered by lax monetary policy heated up. The result was excessively inflated asset prices and reckless overlending by banks (the so-called bubble economy, or *baburu keizai*), which left bad debts amounting to trillions of yen and a credit crunch in the aftermath. This was the major cause of *Heisei fukyo* (the "recession" of the

Heisei era) —the longest period of sluggish growth in Japan's postwar
history. Thus, the numerous costs of the aftermath of the Louvre
coordination are presumed to far outweigh the possible benefits.

The fiscal priorities in the first term of the Reagan administration were
threefold: massive defense buildup, tax cuts, and a balanced budget. But
these three goals were not reconcilable unless non-defense spending or
entitlements could be cut drastically. Despite Reagan's avowed fiscal
conservatism, the balanced budget was the first to go. In David Stockman's
words, "The Reagan Revolution. . .required a frontal assault on the
American welfare state. That was the only way to pay for the Kemp-Roth tax
cut. . . . The true Reagan Revolution never had a chance. It defied all of the
overwhelming forces, interests, and impulses of American democracy."[31]
Thus, taxes were cut, defense spending was increased, and budget deficits
ballooned year by year. Table 3.3 shows this trajectory.

Table 3.3. **U.S. current account balance and government
deficits as percentage of GNP**

Year	Current account	Budget deficits
1981	0.3	1.0
1982	-0.1	3.4
1983	-1.0	4.1
1984	-2.5	2.9
1985	-2.9	3.1
1986	-3.3	3.4
1987	-3.4	2.5
1988	-2.4	2.0

Source: *Economic Report of the President* (Washington, D.C.: GPO,1995).

Current account deficits also increased in tandem.[32] By statistical
identity, external deficits equal the internal saving-investment gap. If the
public sector is "dis-saving" (running a deficit), the country is bound to run
current account deficits unless private savings outweigh private investment
(which is rarely the case in the United States).

The American twin deficits, however, could have been a matter of purely
domestic concern, since the chronic surplus countries—Japan and Germany
(until reunification)—were less concerned about their surpluses. But there
was one more ominous side effect of growing deficits: heightened
protectionism in the United States. American workers vented their anger by
smashing Japanese radios and cars on the street. American industries were
filing complaints with the federal government in record numbers. In
responding to pressures from their constituencies, members of Congress
were sponsoring record numbers of protectionist bills.

After winning reelection, the Reagan administration devised a new strategy of exchange rate cooperation and monetary policy coordination under the leadership of James A. Baker III (formerly chief of staff at the White House) at the helm at the Treasury. The central idea of exchange rate cooperation was to devalue the dollar, which had been considered overvalued. The result was the Plaza Agreement of September 22, 1985. The glass was half full and half empty, however. While it is true that the dollar began to decline very rapidly and the overvaluation problem was therefore corrected, the American current account deficits showed no sign of improvement for a while, presumably due to the J-curve effect.

From then on, the G7's strategy increasingly shifted to coordination of domestic monetary policy. The initiative for coordinating interest rates came from Japan: addressing the Economic Policy Council, an advisory body, on December 18, 1985, Prime Minister Yasuhiro Nakasone advocated coordinated reductions in interest rates in Japan and the United States, declaring that if interest rates were cut all at once, "Bang! Bang!" the world would be better off.[33] Under political pressure, the Bank of Japan cut the discount rate in January. Some members on the Board of Governors at the Federal Reserve were anxious to cut interest rates in the spring in the face of an economic slowdown, and after the so-called Palace Coup on February 24, 1986, when the Board voted to cut the target for the federal funds rate, a benchmark for U.S. monetary policy. Chairman Paul Volcker called his Japanese and German counterparts to ask them to join the United States in cutting interest rates to boost domestic demand. They readily agreed, and coordinated cuts in interest rates were announced on March 6 and 7. And then, the United States and Japan simultaneously cut their interest rates in the following month as well.

The summer of 1986 was a season of politics. The Liberal Democratic Party, facing simultaneous elections in both houses of the Diet, preferred another interest-rate cut. But political pressure on the Bank of Japan (BOJ) was ineffective because "the BOJ united against rate cuts near election time traditionally and single-mindedly."[34]

From then on, the Bank of Japan, along with the German Bundesbank, strenuously resisted political pressure emanating both from inside and from abroad to ease monetary policy further. But the Japanese and German central banks were in a terrible dilemma: the yen and the mark were appreciating far too quickly, and additional rate cuts were necessary to stem their further climb; at the same time, by summer, the money supply was increasing at an alarming rate, and the central banks did not want to ignite inflationary pressure. Thus, even though the Federal Reserve cut federal funds target rates in July and August, neither the BOJ nor the Bundesbank went along.

From then on, American pressure on Japan and Germany grew more intense. In August, Volcker met with his German counterpart, Karl Otto Pöhl, in Frankfurt to demand further interest cuts in Germany; in return Pöhl demanded that the United States cooperate in stabilizing the dollar at about the DM 2.00 level. The bargain was not struck, however.

Japan's attitude was changing partly because Kiichi Miyazawa, whose internationalist and Keynesian leanings were well known, became finance minister in August. He arranged a secret meeting with James Baker in San Francisco on September 6, at which Baker demanded boosting domestic demand in Japan. Miyazawa agreed, but also sought U.S. help in stabilizing the dollar exchange rate. They met later again to arrange a meeting between Volcker and BOJ governor Sumita. Sumita was still reluctant to ease Japanese monetary policy further, but the Ministry of Finance resorted to pressure tactics in October, and the BOJ finally caved in. At the time the Miyazawa-Baker Accord was announced on October 31, the BOJ also revealed that the discount rate would be cut from 3.5 to 3 percent. For a while the dollar-yen rate stabilized around the 160 yen/dollar level, but in January, the yen began to appreciate again. In desperation, Miyazawa flew to Washington to see Baker, but this underprepared meeting produced no result. Baker, for his part, was interested at this time only in applying pressure on Germany, to strike a G7 agreement.[35]

The United States also gained a strong ally around this time. Finance Minister Eduard Balladur openly welcomed the Miyazawa-Baker Accord of October 1986. He, too, was keen to see the dollar stabilized, as he said: "It was a priority for me to examine this possibility with my European colleagues."[36]

Thus, by this time, room for mutual gains was emerging. Japan, France, and, to a lesser extent, Germany were eager to stabilize the exchange rates roughly at the levels of early 1987. Baker was willing to agree to this only insofar as Japan and Germany agreed to further measures of domestic economic stimulus, fiscal or monetary. Since Miyazawa and Stoltenberg were worried about the contracting impact of the sharp appreciation of the their currencies on their economies, they were willing to sacrifice their fiscal stance a little and accede to U.S. pressure. Thus, the result was the Louvre Accord. On February 22 the finance ministers from six of the G7 countries (Italy boycotted the meeting) declared that "they agreed to cooperate closely to foster stability of exchange rates around current levels." Japan agreed that a comprehensive economic program should be prepared "to stimulate domestic demand," adding that the Bank of Japan had announced that it would reduce its discount rate by a half percentage point on February 23. The German government proposed to "increase the size of tax reductions already enacted for 1988." Germany monetary policy would be "directed at improving the conditions for sustained economic growth while maintaining price stability."[37]

In keeping with this broad agreement on exchange rates and macroeconomic policies, Japan stayed the course while expecting the Federal Reserve to keep a tight rein on U.S. monetary policy. It was a gamble. The Bank of Japan was certainly concerned about the sharp appreciation of the yen—40 percent in less than a year and a half—and its effect on the real economy. Indeed, by this time, BOJ governor Sumita was under security surveillance by local police.[38] By mid-1987 the side effects of easy money were clearer: the Nikkei 225 Index was 8,800 yen (average) in 1983; it doubled to 16,400 yen by 1986; it climbed to 26,600 yen by October 1987. Land prices in Tokyo doubled in the two-year period 1986-87 (see Figure 3.15).[39] This was the beginning of the so-called bubble economy. Speculative buying and reselling was becoming rampant in stock, real estate, and other asset markets.

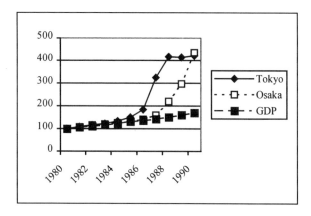

Figure 3.15. **Land prices of commercial areas in Tokyo and Osaka (1980=100)**
Source: Yukio Noguchi, *Baburu no Keizaigaku* (Tokyo: Nihon Keizai Shimbunsha, 1992).

The situation was similar in Germany. Glimpsing inflationary pressures, the Bundesbank switched its monetary stance to one of slight tightening in the summer. The Bank of Japan also began to induce market interest rates to slide higher. The BOJ was prepared to raise its discount rate after the Federal Reserve did so in September. But tightening was nipped in the bud because of Black Monday. Baker, enraged by German monetary tightening, lashed out on October 14. Early that morning, the market had learned that the German Bundesbank was nudging the Repo rate from 3.75 to 3.85 percent.[40] Next, at 8:30 A.M. the Commerce Department announced a whopping August U.S. trade deficit of $15.7 billion. At 3:30 P.M. the newswires reported that Treasury Secretary Baker had attacked the Bundesbank for raising interest rates. The stock market plunged with the dollar. On Friday the dollar fell through the Louvre floor for the dollar-mark rate. The Dow index dropped 108 points. Then came Black Monday (October 19). Baker went to Europe for his previously arranged trip but he decided to make a stopover in Frankfurt to meet with Stoltenberg and Pöhl. That same day, the Dow dropped 508 points or 22.6 percent, the biggest percentage drop in history, worse even than that of Black Thursday (October 24, 1929). All the major stock exchanges the world over followed suit. Baker tried in vain to patch up the crack in G7 cooperation. In the end, it was the Fed-orchestrated rescue operations that saved the world equity markets from a disastrous meltdown. Thus, because of the intervention of Black Monday, Japan missed another opportunity for monetary tightening. A crack in G7 cooperation did not help matters. Finally, the foreign exchange crisis was laid to rest by the Christmas "telephone" agreement of December 22, 1987.

Nineteen eighty-eight ushered in a better year for the G7. The Christmas agreement finally ended the bear market, and the dollar firmed up nicely. The U.S. trade deficit, too, finally turned a corner. Third, the trade war that had begun the previous year between the United States and Japan was subsiding slowly but surely. James Baker was no longer pressuring for further reflation. Thus, the Bank of Japan could at last have turned its attention to the potential ill effects of the bubble economy, but it did not. The discount rate remained at the historic low of 2.5 percent throughout the year. This is a striking contrast to Germany, which had raised the discount rate twice, in July and August 1988, by a half percentage point each.

It is not clear whether the maintenance of the easy monetary stance in Japan was due to international commitment or to its own concern about the exchange rates. In the minds of most Japanese, however, these factors were indistinguishable. Yoshio Suzuki, a former executive director of the BOJ, believes that it was at least partly due to international cooperation.[41] There was also a news report that the Fed and the BOJ had entered into an agreement in which the BOJ would keep interest rates low, which would keep the interest spread between the United States and Japan wide enough to encourage Japanese investment into the U.S.[42] By now it has become orthodoxy in Japan that easy monetary policy at this time was at least one of the major permissive conditions for the bubble economy. BOJ governor Yasuo Matsushita, for instance, testifying before the upper house of the Diet in April 1996, attributed the bubble economy to long-term easing of monetary policy, which was undertaken in light of international cooperation in maintaining exchange rate stability and correcting external imbalances.[43]

6. EVALUATION OF ALTERNATIVE MODELS

As with the previous case, the Louvre Accord supports all the models of counterproductive cooperation to some extent.

6.1. The Rogoff Model

This case certainly follows the outlines of the Rogoff model. International monetary policy coordination certainly led to very loose monetary policy in Japan, which led to the bubbles in asset markets, if not to goods price inflation.

However, there are a few weaknesses. First, it is not clear whether Japan kept a loose monetary policy under international commitment. It is true that some BOJ sources attribute its easy monetary policy to international commitment. But its policy was largely dictated by the goal of exchange rate stability, which in turn was imposed on it by relatively narrow domestic interests.

Second, goods-price inflation did not happen. Only the prices of assets such as real estate and stock were inflated. It could also be argued that easy monetary policy is only a weak permissive condition—but not a sufficient condition—for financial bubbles. For instance, it is sometimes perceived that monetary policy coordination in 1927 led to bubbles in stock and real estate markets in the United States, but Galbraith dismisses this hypothesis: "There were times before and there have been long periods since when credit was plentiful and cheap—far cheaper than than in 1927-29—and when speculation was negligible."[44] Thus, the link between international monetary policy coordination and asset price inflation or bubbles is a tenuous one.

6.2. The Feldstein Model

As we have seen, Feldstein points out that the fiscal authorities both in the U.S. and in Japan have perverse incentives that can seriously distort the proper conduct of monetary policy: first, they may try to put the blame of economic mismanagement on foreigners and central bankers; second, they may try to divert the burden on adjustment to monetary policy. If most proper adjustment should be done through fiscal policy in reality, these incentives could lead to mismanagement of monetary policy and monetary cooperation. Evidence in support of both points was evident in the Louvre case. Thus, James Baker shifted the adjustment burden to foreigners in 1986 and 1987. And in the summer of 1987, when the Bundesbank was dragging its feet on monetary easing, Baker appealed to international public opinion:

With respect to Germany in particular, you are looking at unemployment around 9 percent, you are looking at a negative inflation rate and negative growth. We need some help. We have carried, to a large degree, the world economy for the last 42 or 43 months. . . . We would like to see some help over there.[45]

True to form, the Japanese Ministry of Finance also tried to put the burden of adjustment onto the Bank of Japan in 1986. The clandestine decision to cut the discount rate in October 1986, while BOJ governor Sumita was away, was a characteristic way of passing the buck in Japan.

But it is not coordination but the lack thereof between Japanese fiscal and monetary policies that explains the subsequent series of policy errors. Despite the fact that the Japanese economy was back on track by the spring of 1987, the Ministry of Finance, by caving in to business and LDP pressures, injected a fiscal stimulus of six trillion yen. Combined with already easy monetary policy, this added to land speculation, because most additional spending went to public works. Furthermore, not only monetary tightening by the new BOJ governor Yasushi Mieno, but also quantitative restrictions on real-estate-purchase credit announced by the MOF in 1990 triggered a sudden puncture of the bubbles. Such a simultaneous brake on speculation was worse than the disease itself.

6.3. Model Uncertainty

Both Rogoff and Feldstein paint an image of a politically powerless Bank of Japan caving in to the malicious pressures from the United States, the LDP, and the MOF. This in turn implies that the Bank of Japan could have conducted its monetary policy more judiciously if it had been left to its own devices.[46] This conclusion should be tempered by the fact that economists at the Bank of Japan experienced considerable uncertainty as to the proper course of monetary policy during the period of yen appreciation.

There were several technical questions about which the Bank of Japan was unsure. First, to what extent should the money supply and the inflation indicators influence monetary policy?[47] From 1986 to 1990, the money supply (M2+CD) experienced double-digit growth, but price inflation was relatively moderate. This put the Bank of Japan in a quandary: fast monetary growth suggested early tightening of monetary policy, but the lack of price inflation also meant that monetary policy should be easy enough to allow fast recovery from the "yen appreciation-induced recession" (*endaka fukyo*).

Further, the Bank of Japan did not know the extent to which asset price stability should guide monetary policy.[48] There was no noticeable price inflation in Japan in this period, but by 1987 asset price inflation was more than obvious. If asset price stability had been included in the final policy goals of monetary policy, the Bank of Japan could have started tightening earlier, but because the BOJ was uncertain about the role of asset prices, easy monetary policy continued unchecked.

Thus, these uncertainties in monetary know-how were partly to blame for policy mistakes in Japan during the post-Louvre Accord period. But note that these uncertainties differ somewhat from the kind of uncertainty about international transmission effects that Frankel pointed out. Rather, they were purely domestic policy uncertainties, which could have derailed monetary policy, even without international cooperation. The moral of this episode is that monetary policy is an extremely difficult instrument to manage even without international political entanglements.

6.4. Coercion

James Baker and other policymakers certainly resorted to psychological warfare by talking down the dollar. Like Blumenthal, Baker seemed to have started quite innocently. But he soon realized that the "dollar weapon" could be used strategically. After a few suspected talking-down incidents, however, he became more cautious. But even these few instances left indelible scars on the tissue of international monetary relations. Toyoo Gyohten, the then vice minister of finance, indicted American chauvinism with remarkable frankness:

> On the American side, policymakers came to believe that the best and only way to deal with Japan was to apply pressure: they used the *blackmail of dollar depreciation* and the threat of protectionism, while ignoring that part of the problem resided in the failure of the United States to do what it was supposed to do to correct its own fiscal excesses.[49]

This does not mean that everything was decided by American pressure. Moreover, some of the "crime" in question may have been simply a product of amateurism, a cacophony of different domestic interests, signaling, and the usual dose of egotism. Like beauty, however, coercion is always in the eye of the beholder.

7. CONCLUSIONS

These two cases—the Bonn summit agreement and the Louvre Accord—of seemingly counterproductive cooperation fit all the theories that were outlined in the previous chapter, albeit with some important discrepancies.

Both cases could have been inflationary as in the Rogoff model, but at least the Louvre Accord did not lead to goods-price inflation as predicted by the model. The Bonn summit certainly increased budget deficits in Japan, but it is not clear whether this was worsened because of the international agreement or just a continuation of the trend that had started before.

There is evidence of American coercion (or at least enormous political pressure) on Germany and Japan in both cases, though it was more of a mix of innocence and conspiracy. But to the extent that the intention of coercion was perceived, it seemed to have contributed to their distrust of U.S. sincerity and hence to the perception of policy failure.

Overall, the perspective that seems universally useful is that of model uncertainty. Policymakers faced no small dose of uncertainty about the soundness of proposed plans in both cases; thus, it is no surprise that some policy mistakes were committed along the way. It was not the lack of a vision or strategy but a lack of contingency plans (which are highly advisable in such uncertain situations) and the resulting muddling-through tactics that led to incoherent policy-making and regret afterward.

APPENDIX

Using the coding of U.S. pressure on Japan described in this chapter, we can conduct some additional tests of the models of counterproductive policy coordination.

First, the Rogoff model can be indirectly tested as follows. One of the model's crucial assumptions is that monetary policymakers try to achieve an unemployment level below the natural rate. Otherwise, the inflationary bias of discretionary monetary policy would be unlikely to figure prominently. Under what conditions, then, will policymakers pursue such an objective? The domestic political economy literature shows that partisanship matters: left-leaning governments tend to pursue low unemployment more aggressively than do right-leaning governments.[50] It can therefore be conjectured that Democratic administrations in the United States will be more aggressive than Republican administrations in seeking monetary policy coordination. We can test this hypothesis by regressing the variable for U.S. pressure for Japanese monetary easing on the dummy variable(s) for Democratic administrations. Since the dependent variable takes only nonnegative integer values on a monthly basis, we estimate Poisson regressions by maximum likelihood.

In Table 3.4 the administration variables are dummy variables, for which the base case is the Bush administration. If the above hypothesis is correct, we should expect to see a positive sign for the coefficients for the dummy variables for the Carter and Clinton administrations. Yet, on the contrary, they take negative signs and are not statistically significant. Indeed, the most extreme cases are the first and second terms of the Reagan administration, the first term being most reticent and the second term being most aggressive in pushing monetary policy coordination. Thus, in fact, ideology does not seem to be a good predictor for a preference for monetary policy coordination.

Table 3.4. **Poisson regression test of the partisanship effect**

Period: January 1977-December 1996
Dependent variable: monthly number of articles in *Nihon Keizai Shimbun* that describe
U.S. policymakers' verbal pressure on Japan to ease monetary policy

Explanatory variable	Coefficient estimate
Constant	-4.8995
	(2.1570)*
Carter	-0.4568
	(0.8542)
Reagan I	-2.4442
	(0.9735)*
Reagan II	0.9688
	(0.4715)*
Clinton	-0.6272
	(0.8036)
Japanese unemployment	0.3900
	(0.8676)
Japanese inflation	0.5526
	(0.2682)*
Japanese current account	0.0458
	(0.0209)*
U.S. unemployment	0.2423
	(0.1930)
U.S. inflation	0.1922
	(0.5989)
U.S. current account	0.047
	(0.0223)
Log likelihood	-109.4425

Note: Heteroskedasticity-consistent standard errors are in parentheses;
* $p < .05$ (two-tailed).

Next we can test the Tabelinni model of fiscal policy coordination by regressing the U.S. pressure on Japanese demand management on election variables because the model predicts that fiscal policy coordination is in part motivated by the government's election-induced myopia. Table 3.5 does not support the hypothesis. The dummy variable for the presidential election year has a negative coefficient, which means that when the U.S. administration is in the midst of an election campaign, it is less prone to engage in fiscal policy coordination with Japan.

Using the same data set, we can also conduct an indirect test for Henning's hypothesis on the "dollar weapon": when the United States makes demands on Japan and Germany to change the course of macroeconomic policy, the American officials apply pressure by letting the dollar depreciate by noninterventionism and by talking down.[51] If this hypothesis is true, the variables coded for U.S. verbal pressures should be negatively correlated with U.S. intervention in foreign exchange. I have regressed a composite U.S. pressure variable (the total number of articles regarding U.S. pressure on Japanese monetary easing and domestic demand expansion) on the dummy variable for U.S. intervention against all currencies and another dummy variable for coordination coded from the *Federal Reserve Bulletin*.[52] The results are reported in Table 3.6. The intervention variable is indeed negatively correlated with U.S. pressure, and the coefficient is statistically significant, but when economic control variables are entered, statistical significance vanishes. Thus, this effect is not as robust.

Table 3.5. **Poisson regression test of the electoral effect**

Period: January 1977-December 1996
Dependent variable: monthly number of articles in *Nihon Keizai Shimbun* that describe
U.S. policymakers' verbal pressures for expansion of the Japanese domestic demand

Explanatory variable	Coefficient estimate
Constant	-3.9951
	(1.4266)*
Election year	-2.0502
	(0.5831)*
Year preceding election	-0.0358
year	(0.3614)
Japanese unemployment	-0.8455
	(0.5473)
Japanese inflation	-0.1288
	(0.2993)
Japanese current account	0.0564
	(0.0145)*
U.S. unemployment	0.4644
	(0.1485)*
U.S. inflation	1.0616
	(0.5785)
U.S. current account	-0.0371
	(0.0175)*
Log likelihood	-142.4657

Note: Heteroskedasticity-consistent standard errors are in parentheses;
*$p < .05$ (two-tailed).

Finally, one can test for Feldstein's "blame avoidance" hypothesis: that U.S. policymakers can avoid electoral sanctions for bad economic performance by blaming foreigners for not cooperating with the United States.[53] U.S. verbal pressure gives the impression that American policymakers are trying to cooperate with Japan and Germany; if Feldstein's hypothesis is correct, the policymakers arm themselves with an excuse for bad economic performance by arguing that it is was the foreign governments that caused the problem by refusing to cooperate. We can test for this effect by regressing presidential popularity ratings on the interaction terms between economic performance variables and the U.S. pressure variable. Suppose, for instance, that inflation goes up at some point. This is expected to hurt presidential popularity, but if this is accompanied by efforts at policy coordination, the administration may be able to avoid blame by implicitly shifting the blame for the domestic economic troubles onto foreigners. I have converted the composite U.S. pressure variable into a dummy variable, multiplied it by three U.S. macroeconomic performance variables-unemployment, inflation, and the current account-and regressed presidential popularity measures (Gallup Poll results) on these variables as well as the interaction terms. The results are shown in Table 3.7. As expected, macroeconomic performance affects presidential popularity: unemployment and inflation decrease the approval rating and increase the disapproval rating. Also, the interaction terms between these variables and the U.S. political pressure dummy variable have coefficient estimates of the opposite signs, indicating that blame avoidance has some effects, but these are not statistically significant. Note that the U.S. pressure dummy by itself hurts presidential popularity to a large degree. Thus, the overall support for the Feldstein hypothesis is weak at best.

Table 3.6. **Poisson regression test of the dollar weapon hypothesis**

Period: January 1977-December 1996
Dependent variable: total monthly number of articles in *Nihon Keizai Shimbun* that describe U.S. policymakers' verbal pressures on Japanese monetary policy and domestic demand expansion

Explanatory variable	Coefficient estimate	Coefficient estimate with control variables
Constant	-0.3553	-3.2904
	(0.1840)	(1.5253)*
U.S. intervention	-0.6562	-0.1006
	(0.2820)*	(0.2774)
U.S. coordination of	0.5126	0.0010
intervention	(0.3225)	(0.3444)
Japanese		-0.5620
unemployment		(0.3996)
Japanese inflation		0.0937
		(0.2589)
Japanese current		0.0449
account		(0.0122)*
U.S. unemployment		0.3309
		(0.1289)*
U.S. inflation		0.7692
		(0.5435)
U.S. current account		-0.0409
		(0.0145)*
Log likelihood	-208.9411	-185.33

Note: Heteroskedasticity-consistent standard errors are in parentheses; * $p < .05$ (two-tailed).

Table 3.1. **OLS regression test of the blame avoidance hypothesis**

Period: January 1977-December 1996
Dependent variables: presidential approval and disapproval ratings according to the Gallup Polls

Explanatory variable	Dependent variable: approval rating	Dependent variable: disapproval rating
Constant	13.4290	-4.2503
	(4.7026)*	(3.1708)
Dependent variable (t-1)	0.8703	0.8767
	(0.0362)*	(0.0352)*
Dummy for U.S. pressure	-9.6868	11.4891
(t-1)	(5.9793)	(5.5742)*
U.S. inflation (t-1)	-3.5369	3.9234
	(1.4602)*	(1.3734)*
U.S. inflation × pressure	4.3887	-3.8026
dummy (t-1)	(2.3302)	(2.2715)
U.S. unemployment	-0.6145	0.8451
	(0.3730)	(0.3842)*
U.S. unemployment ×	0.7325	-0.9841
pressure dummy (t-1)	(0.7435)	(0.7011)
U.S. current account (t-1)	0.0286	-0.0495
	(0.0396)	(0.0455)
U.S. current account ×	-0.0786	0.0854
pressure dummy (t-1)	(0.0480)	(0.0501)
R squared	0.802	0.819
Adjusted R squared	0.795	0.813
Durbin-Watson	2.108	2.024

Note: Heteroskedasticity-consistent standard errors are in parentheses;
* $p < .05$ (two-tailed).

NOTES

[1] For instance, Gerald Holtham points out that the Germans tend to believe that the Bonn summit of 1978 added to inflationary pressures. See Holtham, "German Macroeconomic Policy and the 1978 Bonn Economic Summit," in Richard N. Cooper, et al. *Can Nations Agree? Issues in International Economic Cooperation* (Washington, D.C.: Brookings Institution, 1989), 141.

[2] Indeed, in the 1980s, foreign pressure was always in the direction of requesting a reduction in U.S. budget deficits.

[3] For a more precise definition of the coding rules, see Keisuke Iida, "Strategic Actors or Passive Reactors? The Political Economy of U.S.-Japanese Monetary Relations," in Randolph M. Siverson, ed., *Strategic Politicians, Institutions, and Foreign Policy* (Ann Arbor: University of Michigan Press, 1998): 111-12. For a similar approach to the U.S. administration's pressure on the Fed, see Thomas Havrilesky, "Monetary Policy Signaling

from the Administration to the Federal Reserve," *Journal of Money, Credit, and Banking* 20, 1 (February 1988): 83-101.

[4] See, for instance, " Plea by U.S. on Rate Cut Rejected," *New York Times*, April 29, 1991, D1, 4.

[5] Even outside Germany and Japan, criticisms of this coordination episode have been voiced. For instance, OECD states that "the overall picture of this episode is one in which expansionary policies were pursued for too long, resulting in an acceleration of inflation to politically intolerable levels, which in turn necessitated a decisive shift to restrictive monetary policy and subsequent recession." See Organization for Economic Cooperation and Development, *Why Economic Policies Change Course: Eleven Case Studies* (Paris: OECD): 33. But negative assessments predominantly come from the above two countries.

[6] I. M. Destler and Hisao Mitsuyu, "Locomotives on Different Tracks: Macroeconomic Diplomacy, 1977-1979," in I. M. Destler and Hideo Sato, eds., *Coping with U.S.-Japanese Economic Conflicts* (Lexington, Mass.: Lexington Books, D. C. Heath and Company, 1982): 246.

[7] Not-for-attribution interview, November 1989.

[8] Robert D. Putnam and C. Randall Henning, "The Bonn Summit of 1978: A Case Study in Coordination," in Richard N. Cooper et al. *Can Nations Agree? Issues in International Economic Cooperation* (Washington, D.C.: Brookings Institution): 36-37.

[9] Ibid., 35-36.

[10] *The Times* (London), March 2, 1977.

[11] *Business Week*, June 26, 1978, 92-96.

[12] *Financial Times*, July 1, 1977.

[13] Destler and Mitsuyu, "Locomotives on Different Tracks," 248.

[14] Putnam and Henning, "The Bonn Summit of 1978," 49.

[15] *New York Times*, June 16, 1977.

[16] *New York Times*, August 7, 1977.

[17] Putnam and Henning, "The Bonn Summit of 1978," 45.

[18] Ryutaro Komiya and Miyako Suda, *Gendai Kokusai Kin'yuron: Rekishi Seisakuhen* (Tokyo: Nihon Keizai Shimbunsha, 1983): 231.

[19] Destler and Mitsuyu, "Locomotives on Different Tracks," 252.

[20] See *Nihon Keizai Shimbun*, December 16, 1977.

[21] *Financial Times*, May 11, 1978.

[22] G. John Ikenberry, *Reasons of State: Oil Politics and the Capacity of American Government* (Ithaca, NY: Cornell University Press, 1988): 187. Ikenberry interprets the Bonn agreement to be an "outcome of a momentary 'international coalition' of political leaders, each with domestic political problems, each agreeing to create the convenient fiction that hard-fought concessions had been won" (p. 181).

[23] Anthony Solomon, "A Personal Evaluation," in George de Menil and Anthony M. Solomon, *Economic Summitry* (New York: Council on Foreign Relations, 1983): 45.

[24] Toyoo Gyohten, in Paul A. Volcker and Toyoo Gyohten, *Changing Fortunes: The World's Money and the Threat to American Leadership* (New York: Times Books, 1992): 161; emphasis added.

[25] Holtham, "German Macroeconomic Policy," 172.

[26] Ronald I. McKinnon, "Currency Substitution and Instability in the World Dollar Standard," *American Economic Review* 72, 3 (June 1982): 320-33.

[27] See Henry N. Goldstein and Stephen E. Hayes, "A Critical Appraisal of McKinnon's World Money Supply Hypothesis," *American Economic Review* 74, 1 (March 1984): 217-

24; Steven Ambler and Ronald McKinnon, "U.S. Monetary Policy and the Exchange Rate: Comment," *American Economic Review* 75, 3 (June 1985), 557-59.

[28] Interview, Frankfurt, February 7, 1989. Matthöfer attests that skepticism about the locomotive theory was unanimous in Bonn.

[29] Stephen D. Cohen and Ronald I. Meltzer, *United States International Economic Policy in Action: Diversity of Decision Making* (New York: Praeger, 1982), 19.

[30] *Kinyu Zaisei Jijo*, October 31, 1977, 12, cited in Komiya and Suda, *Gendai Kokusai Kinyuron*, 240.

[31] David A. Stockman, *The Triumph of Politics: How the Reagan Revolution Failed* (New York: Harper & Row, 1986): 8-9.

[32] This is not to say that the current account and the budget deficit move on a one-to-one basis.

[33] Yoichi Funabashi, *Managing the Dollar: From the Plaza to the Louvre* (Washington, D.C.: Institute for International Economics, 1988): 45.

[34] Ibid., 51.

[35] There was a flurry of activity between the U.S. and Germany in December and January. David Mulford, undersecretary of the Treasury for international affairs, pressed Germany for reflation at the G5 deputy meeting in Paris, to lay the groundwork for a meeting between Baker and Stoltenberg, German finance minister in Kiel on December 14. Stoltenberg sent Tietmeyer, vice minister of finance, to Washington to meet with Treasury Deputy Secretary Darman. None of these meetings led to a meeting of mind, but nevertheless, German attitudes gradually softened. See Funabashi, *Managing the Dollar*, 172-173; Keisuke Iida, *The Theory and Practice of International Policy Coordination*, Unpublished Ph.D. dissertation (Cambridge: Department of Government, Harvard University, 1990): 466-67.

[36] *Le Monde*, November 20, 1986, the author's translation. Also see Edouard Balladur, *Passion et longuer de temps: Dialogues avec Jean-Pierre Elkabach* (Paris: Fayard, 1989).

[37] For the text of the Louvre Accord communiqué, see Funabashi, *Managing the Dollar*, 277-80.

[38] Satoshi Sumita, *Wasuregataki Hibi 75-nen* (The Unforgettable Days—75 Years)(Tokyo: Kinyu Zaisei Jijo Kenkyukai, 1992): 113-14.

[39] Yukio Noguchi, *Baburu no Keizaigaku: Nihon Keizai ni Naniga Okottanoka* (Tokyo: Nihon Keizai Shimbunsha, 1992): 96-98.

[40] The following description of the sequence of events is based on Steven Solomon, *The Confidence Game* (New York: Simon and Schuster, 1995): 49-50.

[41] Yoshio Suzuki, *Nihon no Kinyu Seisaku* (Tokyo: Iwanami Shoten, 1993): 94-100. He writes: "The triumph of policy coordination was the beginning of the tragedy that mired the Japanese economy in bubbles" (p. 94), the author's translation.

[42] *Nihon Keizai Shimbun*, May 13, 1988.

[43] *Nihon Keizai Shimbun*, April 17, 1996.

[44] John Kenneth Galbraith, *The Great Crash 1929* with a new introduction (Boston: Houghton Mifflin, 1988, originally published in 1954): 11.

[45] *Financial Times*, July 14, 1986.

[46] Indeed, it is because of this lesson that the Japanese government finally decided to grant greater policy independence to the Bank of Japan in 1997.

[47] See Suzuki, *Nihon no Kinyu Seisaku*, 141.

[48] Ibid., 146-50.

[49] Gyohten in Volcker and Gyohten, *Changing Fortunes*, 271; emphasis added.

[50] Alberto Alesina, "Politics and Business Cycles in Industrial Democracies," *Economic Policy* 8 (April 1989): 55-98; Alberto Alesina, John Londregan, and Howard Rosenthal, "A Model of the Political Economy of the United States," *American Political Science Review* 87, 1 (March 1993): 12-33; Alberto Alesina and Howard Rosenthal, "Partisan Cycles in Congressional Elections and the Macroeconomy," *American Political Science Review* 83, 2 (June 1989): 373-98; idem, *Partisan Politics, Divided Government, and the Economy* (New York: Cambridge University Press, 1995); Alberto Alesina and Jeffrey Sachs, "Political Parties and Business Cycle in the United States, 1948-84," *Journal of Money, Credit, and Banking* 20,1 (February 1988): 63-82; Douglas A. Hibbs, Jr., "Political Parties and Macroeconomic Policy," *American Political Science Review* 71, 4 (December 1977): 1467-87; idem, *The American Political Economy: Macroeconomics and Electoral Politics* (Cambridge: Harvard University Press, 1987); idem, *The Political Economy of Industrial Democracies* (Cambridge: Harvard University Press, 1987); Edward R. Tufte, *Political Control of the Economy* (Princeton: Princeton University Press, 1978).

[51] C. Randall Henning, *Macroeconomic Diplomacy in the 1980s: Domestic Politics and International Conflict among the United States, Japan, and Europe*, Atlantic Paper 65 (London: Croom Helm, 1987).

[52] This coordination variable includes coordination with countries other than Japan.

[53] Martin Feldstein, "Thinking about International Economic Coordination," *Journal of Economic Perspectives* 2, 2 (Spring 1988): 3-13.

Chapter 4

Ineffective and Counterproductive Intervention

1. INTRODUCTION

Coordinated intervention in the foreign exchange market has been another important element of G7 cooperation since the 1970s. It has been the object of two different kinds of critique. The first class of arguments, an "ineffectiveness thesis," holds that foreign exchange intervention, whether coordinated or not, is largely ineffective for the following three reasons: (1) intervention is mostly sterilized, (2) the market volume is vast and (3) signaling (intervention as a signal of future monetary policy) does not work. The second class of critique, a "counterproductiveness thesis," goes further and argues that intervention can exacerbate the very problem that it is supposed to cure. Compared to the literature on monetary policy coordination, the counterproductiveness thesis is a distinct minority, but to the extent that it concerns counterproductive international cooperation, it needs to be examined. The following examination shows that this area also suffers from a considerable degree of model uncertainty, which contributes to the perception of the futility of international cooperation.

2. THE INEFFECTIVENESS THESIS

The G7 governments and central banks often intervene in the foreign exchange markets, for various purposes: to smooth daily fluctuations, to guide the exchange rate movement in one direction, and to signal some economic and political stances of the governments. These interventions are not always successful, however. More often than not, they seem to have very negligible influence on the market exchange rates, if any. Partly to reinforce effectiveness of intervention, the G7 central banks also try to coordinate their interventions via telephone communication and through various international meetings. We already saw in the previous chapter that the G5 and G7 governments entered into the Plaza, Louvre, and Christmas agreements in 1985 and 1987 in order to influence the movement of exchange rates. Except for the Christmas agreement of December 1987, coordinated intervention was also perceived to be ineffective for the three main reasons mentioned above: sterilization, market volume, and ineffective signals.

2.1. Sterilization

Foreign exchange intervention occurs when official agents such as the central banks trade foreign exchange on the market. Economists distinguish between sterilized and unsterilized foreign exchange intervention: unsterilized intervention changes the money supply whereas sterilized intervention does not affect the money supply in the domestic financial system. Specifically, sterilized intervention takes place if the central bank conducts open-market operations to offset the money supply effects of intervention.

To illustrate how this works, suppose that the Federal Reserve Bank of New York sells one billion dollars worth of deutsche mark in the foreign exchange markets. The counterparties (typically private banks) that bought the mark now have one billion dollars less in their reserves at the Fed because they have paid that much for the foreign exchange they purchased. That means that high-powered money (which consists of commercial banks' reserves at the central bank as well as coins and bills in circulation) has contracted by one billion dollars. The result will be a tightening of monetary policy, which then affects the exchange rate, both nominal and real, in a significant way. But central banks usually do not like the effects of foreign exchange intervention on the money supply and therefore conduct offsetting open-market operations. So, in the above example, the Fed in its regular operations will buy one billion dollars worth of Treasury bills from private banks. With this operation one billion dollars worth of domestic currency will flow back to the private banking system, leaving the money supply undisturbed.

Economists are unanimous that unsterilized intervention is effective: as long as foreign exchange intervention changes the money supply, it is presumed to affect the exchange rate. On the other hand, most economists are quite skeptical about the effectiveness of sterilized intervention.

The question is the extent to which G7 intervention is sterilized. The empirical estimation is fraught with difficulties, but estimates are typically over 70 percent.[1] Paul Volcker says as follows:

> Almost every central bank has its own objectives for monetary policy, and they are not framed in terms of the amount of foreign exchange intervention. If that intervention either enlarges or contracts the monetary base, the natural instinct is to offset it by domestic monetary actions. In other words, they automatically sterilize intervention to the extent they can. That is the way the Federal Reserve behaves, and so does practically every central bank in countries with well-enough-developed money markets to permit large offsetting operations.[2]

2.2. Market Size and the Portfolio Effect

Economists identify two principal channels through which sterilized intervention influences foreign exchange markets: the portfolio effect and the signaling effect. The portfolio effect obtains when securities of different currencies are not perfect substitutes. In effect, what sterilized intervention does is to change the composition of assets denominated in different currencies in the portfolio of the market agents. For instance, if the Fed buys the dollar for the deutsche mark (thereby contracting the dollar money supply and increasing liquidity in the mark in the hands of banks) but also conducts open market operations to buy dollar-denominated securities in return for cash, the money supply is unchanged, but in the end, the market agents hold more mark-denominated assets and fewer dollar-denominated securities. This may make dollar-denominated assets more attractive in the eye of portfolio managers, who try to keep a certain balance of currency diversification. In this way, sterilized intervention could influence the course of the exchange rate (in the above example, to strengthen the dollar, as is desired by the Fed).[3]

However, the market size is enormous. Especially, in the theory of the portfolio effect, the relevant size is not the volume of daily *flow* of foreign exchange transactions (estimated to be over one trillion dollars worldwide as of 1996), but the stock of dollar-denominated securities, say, in the case of dollar intervention.[4] There are 3.5 trillion dollars worth of marketable U.S. Treasury securities[5] and several trillion dollars worth of highly substitutable corporate bonds outstanding. The central banks' total holdings of foreign reserves are, by contrast, on the order of several tens of billions of dollars, with the exception of the Bank of Japan. Thus, even if the central banks of the U.S., Japan, and Germany spent all their reserves—a highly unlikely event—to influence the dollar exchange rate, they could change private holdings of dollar-denominated securities only by a few percentage points. For this reason, the effectiveness of sterilized intervention through the portfolio effect is presumed to be quite limited.

2.3. Signaling

Signaling is the second channel of influence. The central banks sometimes use intervention to signal the future course of monetary policy. If the market agents correctly perceive such intent, even sterilized intervention can have a powerful effect. Some studies find that the Fed and the Bank of Japan signal their intent through intervention.[6]

But other studies seem to show that this effect is ephemeral at best. Klein and Rosengren, for example, studied the extent to which intervention reflected the future course of monetary policy after the Plaza Agreement.[7] While there is some indication that the markets perceived a signal in the immediate aftermath of the Plaza-Agreement intervention, subsequent monetary policy did not reflect such intent, and therefore the signaling effect of intervention wore off quickly.

This will not come as a surprise to anyone familiar with the making of monetary policy. Intervention policy is often decided quite independently of domestic monetary policy. Even if the policymakers in charge of intervention policy try to use intervention to signal monetary policy, those policymakers in charge of monetary policy may not comply with the wishes. In the United States, for instance, the Treasury Department has authority over intervention policy, but the Fed decides monetary policy, which is independent of the government. Thus, even if the Treasury Department intends to use intervention to signal the Fed's monetary policy, the latter may not follow the course intended by the Treasury.

In summary, many mainstream economists and American policymakers argue that foreign exchange intervention is ineffective because (1) intervention is sterilized, (2) market size is too big for the portfolio effect, and (3) signals about monetary policy are hard to send through intervention.[8]

Although in minority, another critical view exists: that intervention is counterproductive or destabilizing. We'll examine this view next.

3.   DESTABILIZING INTERVENTION

As we saw in chapter 1, Friedman offered the striking insight that speculation is stabilizing as long as speculators buy low and sell high.[9] The corollary is that speculation is destabilizing if speculators sell low and buy high, which becomes obvious if they consistently lose money.

The same logic applies to official intervention: if it is to be stabilizing, the central bank must buy low and sell high, resulting in profits. If, to the contrary, the central bank buys high and sells low, it will lose money over time. The test is deceptively simple.

Dean Taylor conducted this test and found that most central banks of the major industrial countries were losing money, which suggests that their intervention was destabilizing rather than stabilizing, the banks' own contention to the contrary notwithstanding.[10]

Kathryn Dominguez believes that signaling is the major channel of influence of intervention and finds that intervention, if done secretly, can be destabilizing.[11] Indeed, intervention is often secret, with the results that the markets may not perceive the signaling intent correctly and hence may become nervous and unstable. This is an unintended consequence of official intervention.

4. NOMINAL VERSUS REAL EXCHANGE RATES

Finally, there is yet another argument as to why intervention policy is counterproductive, although it concerns intervention less directly than the previous two criticisms. The G7 governments and central banks often target nominal exchange rates assuming that nominal stability is synonymous with real stability. Feldstein argued against targeting nominal exchange rates, however, because real exchange rates can change due to international differences in inflation rates even if nominal exchange rates remain unchanged. Thus, if monetary authorities try to peg nominal exchange rates, the rates may diverge from fundamental equilibrium levels over time, which in turn only exacerbates adjustment problems. As Feldstein argues:

> [T]he political discussion about exchange rate targets, target zones, and exchange rate management are [sic] always in terms of the nominal exchange rates. Therefore, even if the politically agreed upon exchange rate target were achieved and maintained, the relative competitiveness of the countries could change substantially because differences in inflation rates would cause the real exchange rates to change. In short, exchange rate management is likely to be misguided because it focuses on the wrong target.[12]

These criticisms of intervention policy have directly implications for coordination of intervention among the G7 central banks.

5.   A STATISTICAL OVERVIEW

Intervention is a highly secretive affair. Unlike domestic monetary
operations, the central bank rarely announces the timing or the volume of
foreign exchange intervention. Thus, data availability is limited. Indeed,
among the major industrial countries, only the United States reveals the
amount of intervention after the fact. For other countries, analysts still have
to estimate the amount and timing of intervention from various sources. The
trend, however, is in the direction of greater and timelier disclosure, a
welcome development.

By contrast, the data on *coordination* of foreign exchange intervention is
still difficult to come by for several reasons. First, it is not readily clear what
in fact constitutes coordination. Because monetary officials are always in
touch with their counterparts in other major industrial countries,
communication does not seem to be a sufficient criterion for determining
that coordination has occurred. Theoretically, the amount and timing of
coordinated intervention ought to be different from those of noncoordinated
intervention. But those criteria have not been helpful in practice. As a result,
various researchers have had to look to other criteria for empirically
estimating the amount of coordinated intervention.

Bank of Italy economists, for their part, have proposed perhaps the most
rigorous operationalization of G3 (U.S., German, and Japanese) coordination
of foreign exchange intervention as follows: (1) at least two of the G3 central
banks start to intervene together; (2) at least one of these three central banks
continues to intervene with interruptions lasting no more than five working
days; (3) interventions of 20 million dollars or less per day are disregarded;
and (4) episodes that do not include at least two days of simultaneous
intervention or that do not last more than four working days are discarded.[13]
On the basis of these criteria, they identified a total of nineteen episodes of
coordination between 1985 through 1991, constituting probably the most
conservative estimate of G3 coordination.

Iida measured the incidence of coordination on the basis of the verbal
reporting of coordination found in the quarterly report on foreign exchange
intervention published by the Federal Reserve.[14] Coordination was coded on
a monthly basis, and the number of months per year when coordination was
reported is shown in Figure 4.1. According to this estimate, there were two
periods of intense coordination: 1978-80 and 1987-89. These correspond
roughly to the periods of monetary and fiscal policy coordination examined
in Chapter 3.

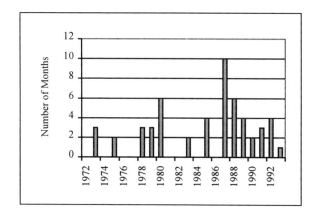

Figure 4.1. **Frequency of coordinated U.S. intervention**
Source: *Federal Reserve Bulletin*

Finally, Dominguez adopted the most expansive operationalization of coordination, identifying intervention as coordinated if two or all of the G3 central banks intervened in the same direction (selling or purchasing the dollar) on the same day. By this criterion, the G3 central banks coordinated on 81 out of 760 trading days from 1985 through 1987.

I have reproduced the incidence of coordinated intervention by the Dominguez method for the U.S.-German pair (1977-88) and the U.S.-Japanese pair (1988-93), using unpublished daily Bundesbank and BOJ intervention data. These coordination (dummy) variables are coded on a daily basis. I have converted these data to monthly series and counted the number of months in which coordination among these pairs of central banks occurred. This is by far the most comprehensive coding of G3 coordination of foreign exchange intervention in the literature. Figures 4.2 and 4.3 compares this data with the Bank of Italy and Fed data.

One might wonder whether this most permissive criterion used for defining coordination would tend to overestimate the incidence of G3 coordination. This turns out to be somewhat true for the late 1970s, when the number of coordination months estimated by this method outstrips the Fed reports. But for the late 1980s, using the same data with the Dominguez method yields results that are is highly comparable to one finds with other methods. All the data point to the same conclusions: coordination of foreign exchange interventions among the G3 central banks is highly common, but there are great fluctuations, the peaks being 1978-80 and 1987-89 and the troughs being the early 1970s and early the 1980s.

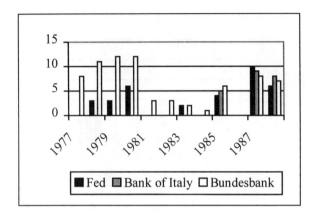

Figure 4.2. **Frequency of coordinated U.S. intervention**
Source: Federal Reserve, Bank of Italy, Bundesbank; Period 1977-88

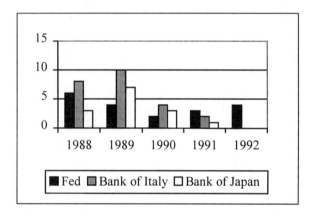

Figure 4.3. **Frequency of coordinated U.S. intervention**
Source: Federal Reserve, Bank of Italy, Bank of Japan; Period 1988-92

Below, I show the results of a simple test for stability properties of intervention by the G3 central banks.[15] On the basis of the Friedman-Taylor idea that stabilizing intervention must buy low and sell high while destabilizing intervention buys high and sells low, we can conduct a more direct test for stabilizing and destabilizing intervention with daily data. For each month, the period-average exchange rate, the average rate only for the days of dollar sales, and that only for the days of dollar purchases by the central bank are calculated. Intervention is deemed stabilizing if and only if the average rate (foreign currency per dollar) for dollar sales is higher than the monthly average and the monthly average is higher than the average rate for dollar purchases. Conversely, intervention is deemed destabilizing if and only if the average rate for dollar sales is lower than the monthly average and the monthly average is lower than the average rate for dollar purchases. Otherwise, intervention is deemed mixed.[16]

Figures 4.4 through 4.7 show the results for all intervention (both coordinated and noncoordinated) by the Federal Reserve, the Deutsche Bundesbank, and the Bank of Japan. The mark-dollar exchange rate is taken from Datastream (Midland Bank's daily mid quote), while the yen-dollar rate is a closing rate in Tokyo, according to the Bank of Japan. Despite some cross-country differences, one can detect some consistent patterns. First, there is some incidence of destabilizing intervention by each of the G3 central banks, though not as frequent as the Taylor results may have implied.[17] Second, the frequency of stabilizing intervention is higher than that of destabilizing intervention. Third, the incidence of mixed intervention is quite high. Thus, one can conclude that G3 intervention overall is neither clearly stabilizing nor destabilizing.

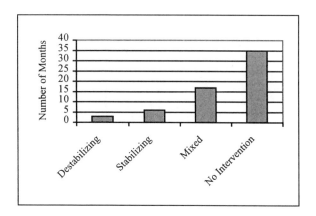

Figure 4.4. **Stability properties of U.S. intervention
(DM vs. U.S. dollar)**
Source: Federal Reserve, Datastream; Period: 1983-88

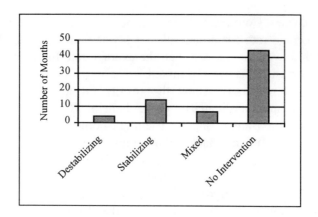

Figure 4.5. **Stability properties of U.S. intervention
(yen vs. U.S. dollar)**
Source: Federal Reserve, Bank of Japan; Period: 1988-93

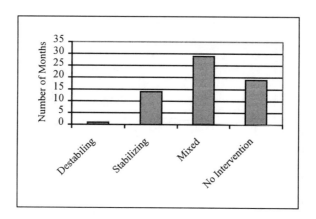

Figure 4.6. **Stability properties of German intervention
(DM vs. U.S. dollar)**
Source: Bundesbank, Datastream; Period: 1983-88

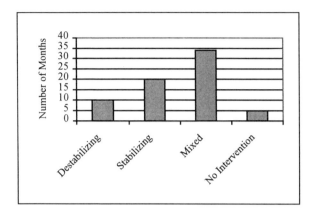

Figure 4.7. **Stability properties of Japanese intervention
(yen vs. U.S. dollar)**
Source: Bank of Japan; Period: 1988-93

Next, using the coding for coordination according to the Dominguez criterion (intervention in the same direction within 24 hours), the incidence of stabilizing and destabilizing nature of *coordinated* intervention was measured. The results are shown in Figures 4.8 through 4.11.

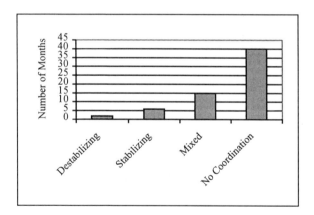

Figure 4.8. **Stability properties of U.S. intervention
coordinated with Germany**
Source: Federal Reserve, Datastream; Period: 1983-88

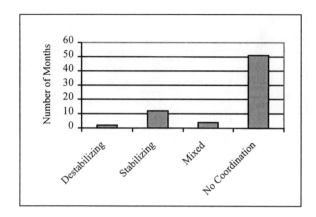

Figure 4.9. **Stability properties of U.S. intervention
coordinated with Japan**
Source: Federal Reserve, Bank of Japan; Period: 1988-93

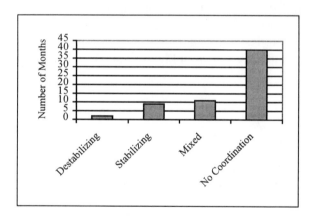

Figure 4.10. **Stability properties of German intervention
coordinated with the United States**
Source: Bundesbank, Datastream; Period: 1983-88

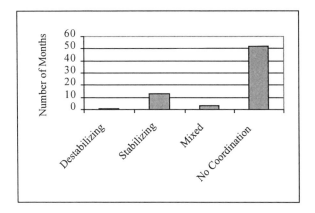

Figure 4.11. **Stability properties of Japanese intervention coordinated with the United States**
Source: Bank of Japan; Period: 1988-93

While the overall patterns are similar to those shown above, there are some differences. Above all, the number of months in which German and Japanese interventions are judged to be mixed is lower when they coordinate with the United States (compare Figures 4.6 and 4.10, Figures 4.7 and 4.11). Thus, coordination has salutary effects because German and Japanese interventions with dubious effects are likely to be restrained by the United States, which is less interventionist than Germany or Japan.

All in all, the data are mixed as to the stabilizing and destabilizing nature of intervention by the G3 countries. While the extreme view that intervention is always counterproductive/destabilizing can be easily rejected, the data do not consistently support the officially stated purpose of smoothing or stabilizing the rate in the short term.

Next, we will conduct a qualitative case study of the policy debate about the effectiveness/counterproductiveness of intervention fought by the G7 countries in the 1980s.

6.   CASE STUDY: INTERVENTION DEBATES IN THE 1980S

During the first term of the Reagan administration, the top leaders of the U.S. Treasury were convinced that market intervention was ineffective and even detrimental to American interests. In April 1981 the Treasury Department announced that it would discontinue the practice of regular intervention in foreign exchange markets and resort to it only under extraordinary circumstances.[18] The Europeans and Japanese immediately attacked this new policy. At the International Monetary Conference (IMC), for example, Karl Otto Pöhl, president of the Bundesbank, asserted: "I want to emphasize that intervention in the exchange market is an instrument, or sometimes a weapon, which we would not give up."[19] The French were by far the most vocal proponents of active intervention policy. In response to strong pressure from the French government to resume active exchange intervention policy, the Americans agreed to study the effects of intervention policy among the governments of the seven major industrial countries, but their skepticism was obvious. Treasury Secretary Donald T. Regan wrote in 1982:

> There have been repeated suggestions for the U.S. government to "intervene" in foreign exchange markets. . . . How any government is to determine a priori what are the proper exchange rates is a question that the critics never quite answer. Foreign exchange rate trends are, by and large, the products of fundamental forces at work in a totally enormous market. The exchange markets handle as much as $40 to 50 billion each day. We believe that, except in cases of a truly disorderly market, government intervention is *futile*. In some cases, it is even *counterproductive*.[20]

The intervention study by the seven governments took more than a year and produced an enormous amount of quantitative and qualitative research, but the results were not enough to pose any challenge to the firm American belief in the futility of intervention.[21] The resulting report reflected compromise rather than genuine agreement and contained many contradictory conclusions. Thus, at one point, the report reflects the American view: "Sterilized intervention did not appear to have constituted an effective instrument in the face of persistent market pressures."[22] And elsewhere it supports the European view: "Sterilized intervention is likely to have a direct impact on exchange rates."[23] The Europeans and Japanese also believed joint intervention involving the United States to be much more effective than uncoordinated intervention. This view is reflected in the conclusions that "the effectiveness of exchange market intervention had been greatly enhanced because of the strong beneficial influence of joint intervention on market psychology."[24]

	United State	
Europe	**Intervention**	**No intervention**
Intervention	Very effective	Moderately effective
No intervention	---	No effect

Figure 4.12. **European view of coordination, 1981-85**

	United States	
Europe	**Intervention**	**No intervention**
Intervention	No effect or counter-productive	No effect or counter-productive
No intervention	---	No effect

Figure 4.13. **U.S. view of coordination, 1981-85**

Figures 4.12 and 4.13 show the European and American views of exchange intervention. The Europeans held joint or coordinated intervention to be the most effective and the preferable method. The United States (the Treasury) considered intervention to be ineffective at best and counterproductive at worst and therefore preferred noninterventionism. With both sides holding to such contrasting views, it is not surprising that the early 1980s saw no cooperation.

Toward the end of 1984 and at the beginning of 1985, the European exchange markets became extremely volatile, and the Europeans engaged in massive intervention in exchange markets. In the face of the pound crisis, the British government lobbied for international cooperation at the G5 meeting in January, with the result that the five governments agreed to coordinate their intervention if necessary.[25] As Regan explained U.S. participation in the agreement: "We are willing to undertake coordinated intervention when we agree that it would be helpful."[26]

However, there is little doubt that the change of American attitudes toward intervention was greatly facilitated by the change of leadership at the U.S. Treasury from Regan and Beryl W. Sprinkel to James A. Baker III and Richard G. Darman, who showed some signs of flexibility on the exchange rate issue. Taking advantage of this window of opportunity, the Europeans sent a strong signal to both the United States government and the markets. Led by the Bundesbank, the European central banks sold more than $10 billion in February and March, checking a further rise in the dollar. In contrast, U.S. participation in this round of intervention was minuscule, and a top-ranking American official said that the winter intervention turned out to be "totally ineffective."[27]

Baker was quite frankly skeptical about intervention at the outset: "It [intervention] does not work because you have a market—the dollar market—that is tremendous in terms of what it used to be."[28] But he was not rigid: "There is 100 to 150 billion dollars traded every day so intervention has to be massive and well coordinated in order to succeed."[29] The last remark suggests that Baker's views differed somewhat from those of his predecessor's. He was also open to innovation: "The interest is solely and exclusively whether or not there is a better way."[30] Further, "We are simply willing to consider, or look at, any new approach that might provide stability."[31]

In response to growing external deficits, partly driven by the strong dollar, and the corresponding rise in protectionism in the United States, Baker directed the Treasury to engineer a secret agreement among the G5 nations to undertake massive coordinated intervention in the foreign exchange markets in the summer of 1985, culminating in the Plaza Agreement of September 22.

It would seem that the Plaza Agreement was an unambiguous success in achieving its stated objective: between February 1985 and December 1986, the dollar depreciated by more than 40 percent in *real terms* against a weighted average of all the major industrial currencies.[32] But this does not mean that the agreement and the subsequent market intervention were unambiguously effective. Indeed, Martin Feldstein, chairman of the Council of Economic Advisors from 1983 to 1985, believes that the Plaza strategy had no durable effect on the value of the dollar:

> The G5 meeting and the subsequent exchange market intervention had no sustained effect on the dollar's overall rate of decline. In the first days after the G5 meeting the dollar declined by about four percent against the other major industrial currencies. But then the dollar resumed its previous

gradual rate of decline. . . . There is simply no evidence in the dollar's behavior since early 1985 to suggest that the G5 meeting and the process of coordinated intervention had any effect on the rate of decline of the dollar's value.[33]

Of course, this does not necessarily represent the official assessment by the U.S. government at that time. Documenting the American assessment at the time is difficult because the American participants in the Plaza Agreement are remarkably reticent about their evaluation of its effectiveness. Only Richard Darman, deputy secretary of the Treasury from 1985 to1987, briefly notes that the period from the Plaza Agreement through the Louvre Accord was "the international equivalent of success with tax reform."[34] Baker devoted his memoirs entirely to his years as secretary of state.[35] Paul Volcker, chairman of the Federal Reserve Board from 1979 to 1987, while bemoaning the excessive volatility of the exchange market, denied that the Plaza Agreement had any impact on monetary policy—an effect that would have made the Plaza intervention more effective: "But the real effect, at the margin, was to reduce the size and likelihood of any easing of monetary policy."[36] Thus, it could be conjectured that the majority view in the U.S. policy circles was either agnostic or skeptical about the success of the Plaza Agreement.

The case study shows that the ineffectiveness and counterproductiveness theses about foreign exchange intervention are not just academic. Some policymakers strongly supported these views in the debates of the 1980s. Of course, the fact that policymakers share these views does not mean that they are correct, but obviously coordination will be rarer than if policymakers believe that intervention is effective and cooperation beneficial.

Nonetheless, the Europeans at the time often enunciated the opposite view that intervention can sometimes be quite effective and coordination useful. The fact that there is no firm consensus on this issue among policymakers endorses the model uncertainty theory: there is great uncertainty about how and to what extent intervention influences the exchange markets. In such a situation, it is not surprising that some policymakers learn a negative lesson that market intervention is ineffective or counterproductive, even though the evidence is not unambiguous by scientific standards.

7. CONCLUSIONS

This chapter reviewed several arguments about official intervention, because much of cooperation among the central banks of the major industrial countries consists of coordination of their intervention in foreign exchange markets. There are three strands of argument: (1) intervention is ineffective; (2) intervention can be destabilizing; and (3) intervention could be counterproductive if monetary authorities target nominal exchange rates instead of real rates.

The case study has shown that all of these have some resonance with actual practice. U.S. policymakers tend to share the ineffectiveness and counterproductiveness theses, thereby endorsing the prescriptive conclusions of such views: noninterventionism. In that case, cooperation is not likely to be practiced. But that does not mean that intervention is truly ineffective or counterproductive. Actually, considerable uncertainty reigns in this issue-area, and as a result, effectiveness and counterproductiveness are a highly subjective matter, colored by the particular ideology, job experience, and career background of policymakers in question.

APPENDIX

Suppose that coordinated foreign-exchange intervention is inherently ineffective or counterproductive but that there is model uncertainty about this fact before a policymaker assumes office. Even with noises in the economy, we would expect policymakers to learn the truth and become increasingly reluctant to cooperate over time. Thus, we can indirectly test for the counterproductiveness/ineffectiveness theses by bypassing the problem of estimating each policymaker's objective function. This appendix conducts this test by using the coding of coordinated intervention, using the Dominguez criterion described in this chapter.

The learning variable used in the test is based on the notion of learning by doing: the more policy experience each policymaker acquires, the more accurate will be the learned information and the more the policymaker will base his subsequent behavior on that information. In particular, the learning variable is operationalized as the cumulative volume of intervention each policymaker experienced since the beginning of his term. The dependent variable is the daily volume of coordinated intervention. Since the dependent variable takes only nonnegative values, Tobit equations are estimated by maximum likelihood. For the United States, the relevant actors are administrations and Treasury secretaries. Although the Federal Reserve conducts actual intervention, the Department of the Treasury is the statutory authority over intervention policy.[37] In Germany both the federal government as a whole and the president of the Bundesbank are considered relevant. Finally, the relevant actors in Japan are assumed to be cabinets (correlated with finance ministers) and the vice minister of finance for international affairs (*zaimukan*), who directs Japanese intervention policy on the operational level.

The results in the following tables are striking. Of sixteen equations successfully estimated with statistically significant coefficients on the learning variable, nine coefficients have a positive sign and seven have a negative sign. A majority of policymakers, that is, became more willing to coordinate their intervention as they experienced more cumulative intervention whereas a substantial proportion of policymakers also had a negative experience for various reasons, including their learning about the apparent ineffectiveness or counterproductiveness of intervention.

Table 4.1. **Tobit regression test of the learning hypothesis: U.S. administrations**

Dependent variable: absolute daily amount of U.S. intervention against all currencies (unit: million U.S. dollars) multiplied by the dummy variable for coordination with Germany (1977-88) or coordination with Japan (1988-93)

Explanatory variable	Carter	Reagan	Bush
Constant	-178.108	-706.077	-256.017
	(16.958)	(66.498)*	(87.858)*
Learning (cumulative intervention)	0.001901	0.01632	-0.029690
	(0.0006161)*	(0.002434)*	(0.004832)*
Sigma squared	47812	125425	282274
	(4648)*	(21426)*	(63367)*
Period	January 1977-Janury 1981	January 1981-December 1988	January 1989-January 1993
Number of observations	1057	2074	1043
Mean log likelihood	-2.09355	-0.494626	-0.570332

Note: Standard errors are in parentheses;
* $p < .05$ (two-tailed).

Table 4.2. **Tobit regression test of the learning hypothesis: U.S. Treasury secretaries**

Dependent variable: same as Table 4.1

Explanatory variable	Blumenthal	Miller	Regan	Baker	Brady
Constant	-204.155	-130.670	-3.52834	-774.207	-391.899
	(20.572)*	(33.139)*	(50.69630)	(97.671)*	(81.582)*
Learning (cumulative intervention)	0.008190	0.000299	-0.178986	0.026355	-0.019467
	(0.001549)*	(0.002834)	(0.040390)*	(0.005166)*	(0.003365)*
Sigma squared	46124	44326	22131	153418	278274
	(5659)*	(7097)*	(7364)*	(33194)*	(57767)*
Period	January 1977-August 1979	August 1979-January 1981	January 1981-February 1985	February 1985-August 1988	August 1988-January 1993
Number of observations	663	384	1055	918	1138
Mean log likelihood	-2.04487	-2.19516	-0.251742	-0.679082	0.621169

Note: Standard errors are in parentheses;
*$p < .05$ (two-tailed).

Table 4.3. **Tobit regression test of the learning hypothesis: Japanese cabinets**

Dependent variable: absolute daily amount of Japanese intervention (unit: million U.S. dollars) multiplied by the dummy variable for coordination with the United States

Explanatory variable	Takeshita	Uno	Kaifu I	Kaifu II
Constant	-1912.97 (377.96)*	460.240 (342.037)	-45.9430 (124.7855)	1888.96 (335.80)*
Learning (cumulative intervention)	0.164428 (0.036957)*	-0.151363 (0.050755)*	-0.050454 (0.015826)*	-0.240914 (0.044050)*
Sigma squared	530609 (186340)*	997049 (441453)*	288827 (91604)*	421771 (198363)*
Period	April 1988- June 1989	June 1989- August 1989	August 1989- February 1990	February 1990- November 1991
Number of observations	289	48	135	418
Mean log likelihood	-0.77900	-2.50974	-1.86670	-0.212868

Note: Standard errors are in parentheses;
* $p < .05$ (two-tailed).

Table 4.4. **Tobit regression test of the learning hypothesis: Japanese vice ministers of finance**

Dependent variable: same as Table 4.3

Explanatory variable	Gyohten	Utsumi
Constant	-1714.04 (294.171)*	-358.590 (168.033)*
Learning (cumulative intervention)	0.062035 (0.013914)*	-0.056481 (0.011031)*
Sigma squared	1011156 (285058)*	956431 (264885)*
Period	April 1988-July 1989	August 1989-July 1991
Number of observations	330	496
Mean log likelihood	-1.10032	-0.762858

Note: Standard errors are in parentheses;
* $p < .05$ (two-tailed).

Table 4.5. **Tobit regression test of the learning hypothesis: German governments**

Dependent variable: absolute daily amount of German intervention (unit: million Deutschemarks) multiplied by the dummy variable for coordination with the United States

Explanatory variable	Schmidt	Kohl
Constant	-114.338	-1919.27
	(17.911)	(207.14)
Learning (cumulative intervention)	-0.003067 (0.000432)*	0.011081 (0.002335)*
Sigma squared	66040	788539
	(6180)*	(135166)*
Period	January 1977-October 1982	October 1982-December 1988
Number of observations	1499	1631
Mean log likelihood	-1.71231	-0.639901

Note: Standard errors are in parentheses;
* $p < .05$ (two-tailed).

Table 4.6. **Tobit regression test of the learning hypothesis: German Bundesbank presidents**

Dependent variable: same as Table 4.5

Explanatory variable	Emminger	Poehl
Constant	-196.497	-789.434
	(24.270)*	(66.724)*
Learning (cumulative intervention)	0.002636 (0.000967)*	-0.001695 (0.000640)*
Sigma squared	57955	407339
	(6506)*	(48901)*
Period	January 1977-December 1979	January 1980-December 1988
Number of observations	781	2349
Mean log likelihood	-2.18737	-0.836328

Note: Standard errors are in parentheses;
* $p < .05$ (two-tailed).

NOTES

[1] See, for instance, Leroy O. Laney and Thomas D. Willett, "International Liquidity Explosion and Worldwide Inflation: The Evidence from Seterilization Coefficient Estimates," *Journal of International Money and Finance* 1, 2 (August 1982): 141-52.

[2] Paul Volcker and Toyoo Gyohten, *Changing Fortunes: The World's Money and the Threat to American Leadership* (New York: Times Books, 1992): 236.

[3] For empirical tests for the portfolio effect, see Atish R. Ghosh, "Is It Signalling? Exchange Intervention and the Dollar-Deutschemark Rate," *Journal of International Economics* 32, 3-4 (May 1992): 201-20; Kathryn M. Dominguez and Jeffrey A. Frankel, "Does Foreign Exchange Market Intervention Matter? The Portfolio Effect," *American Economic Review* 83, 5 (December 1993): 1356-69.

[4] Policymakers, as quoted below, and even some academics are overly impressed by daily flows. Nevertheless, capital liberalization among the major industrial countries has certainly affected the impact of the portfolio effect by rendering securities denominated in different currencies increasingly substitutable. For the historical analysis of capital liberalization among the G7 countries, see Jeffrey A. Frankel, *The Yen/Dollar Agreement: Liberalizing Japanese Capital Markets*, Policy Analyses in International Economics 9 (Washington, D.C.: Institute for International Economics, 1984); John B. Goodman and Louis W. Pauly, "The Obsolescence of Capital Controls? Economic Management in an Age of Global Markets," *World Politics* 46, 1 (October 1993): 50-82; Eric Helleiner, "States and the Future of Global Finance," *Review of International Studies* 18 (1993): 31-49; idem, *States and the Reemergence of Global Finance: From Bretton Woods to the 1990s* (Ithaca, NY: Cornell University Press, 1994). Webb focuses on the impact of increasing capital mobility on G7 cooperation: see Michael C. Webb, "International Economic Structures, Government Interests, and International Coordination of Macroeconomic Adjustment Policies," *International Organization* 45, 3 (Summer 1991): 307-42; idem, *The Political Economy of Policy Coordination: International Adjustment since 1945* (Ithaca, NY: Cornell University Press, 1995).

[5] As of December 1996. See *Economic Report of the President* (Washington, D.C.: Government Printing Office, 1997), Table B-85.

[6] For the Fed, see Graciela L. Kaminsky and Karen K. Lewis, *Does Foreign Exchange Intervention Signal Future Monetary Policy?* Finance and Economics Discussion Series 93-1 (Washington, D.C.: Federal Reserve Board, February 1993); for the Bank of Japan, see Tsutomu Watanabe, *Sijo no Yoso to Keizai Seisaku no Yukosei* (Tokyo: Toyo Keizai Shimposha, 1994).

[7] Michael W. Klein and Eric S. Rosengren, "Foreign Exchange Intervention as a Signal of Monetary Policy," *New England Economic Review* (May/June 1991): 39-50.

[8] The economic literature on the ineffectiveness of intervention is too voluminous to be summarized here. For earlier demonstrations of ineffectiveness, see Maurice Obstfeld, "Exchange Rates, Inflation, and the Sterilization Problem: Germany, 1975-1981," *European Economic Review* 21, 1-2 (March/April 1983): 161-89; Kenneth Rogoff, "On the Effects of Sterilized Intervention: An Analysis of Weekly Data," *Journal of Monetary Economics* 14, 2 (September 1984): 133-50. For a more recent literature, see Geert J. Almekinders, *Foreign Exchange Intervention: Theory and Evidence* (Hants, U.K.: Edward Elgar, 1995); Kathryn M.

Dominguez and Jeffrey A. Frankel, "Does Foreign Exchange Market Intervention Matter? The Portfolio Effect," *American Economic Review* 83, 5 (December 1993):1356-69; idem, Does Foreign Exchange Intervention Work? (Washington, D.C.: Institute for International Economics, 1993); Owen F. Humpage, "Central-Bank Intervention: Recent Literature, Continuing Controversy," *Federal Reserve Bank of Cleveland Economic Review* 27 (Q2 1991): 12-26; Mark P. Taylor, "The Economics of Exchange Rates," *Journal of Economic Literature* 33, 1 (March 1995): 13-47.

[9] Milton Friedman, "The Case for Flexible Exchange Rates," in *Essays in Positive Economics* (Chicago: University of Chicago Press, 1953): 157-203.

[10] Dean Taylor, "Official Intervention in the Foreign Exchange Market, or, Bet against the Central Bank," *Journal of Political Economy* 90, 2 (April 1982): 356-68.

[11] Kathryn M. Dominguez, *Does Central Bank Intervention Increase the Volatility of Foreign Exchange Rates?*, NBER Working Paper 4532 (November 1993).

[12] Martin Feldstein, "Thinking about International Economic Coordination," *Journal of Economic Perspectives* 2, 2 (Spring 1988), 6.

[13] Pietro Catte, Giampaolo Galli, and Salvatore Rebecchini, "Concerted Interventions and the Dollar: An Analysis of Daily Data," in Peter Kenen, Francesco Papadia, and Fabrizio Saccomanni, eds., *The International Monetary System* (Cambridge: Cambridge University Press, 1994): 203.

[14] Keisuke Iida, "The Political Economy of Exchange-Rate Policy: U.S. and Japanese Intervention Policies, 1977-1990," *Journal of Public Policy* 13, 4 (October-December 1993): 327-49; "International Cooperation in Exchange Rate Management: Coordination of U.S. and Japanese Intervention, 1977-1990," *International Interactions* 20, 4 (March 1995): 279-95.

[15] This test is similar but not equivalent to the more common test in the literature: estimation of reaction functions of intervention to exchange rate movements. The literature is almost unanimous that the reaction of the G3 countries to exchange rate movements is predominantly one of leaning against the wind, which is presumably stabilizing. See Almekinders, *Foreign Exchange Intervention*; Jacques R. Artus, "Exchange Rate Stability and Managed Floating: The Experience of the Federal Republic of Germany," *IMF Staff Papers* 23, 2 (July 1976): 312-33; S. C. W. Eijffinger and A. P. D. Gruijters, "On the Short Term Objectives of Daily Intervention by the Deutsche Bundesbank and the Federal Reserve System in the U.S. Dollar -Deutsche Mark Exchange Market," *Kredit und Kapital* 24, 1 (1991): 50-72; Manfred J. M. Neumann, "Intervention in the Mark/Dollar Market: The Authorities' Reaction Function," *Journal of International Money and Finance* 3, 2 (August 1984): 223-40; Peter J. Quirk, "Exchange Rate Policy in Japan: Leaning Against the Wind," *IMF Staff Papers* 24, 3 (November 1977): 642-64; Paul Wonnacott, *U.S. Intervention in the Exchange Market for DM, 1977-80*, Princeton Studies in International Finance 51 (Princeton: International Finance Section, Department of Economics, Princeton University, December 1982).

[16] When the differences were less than a yen per dollar or a pfennig per dollar, the above inequalities were considered to be not satisfied.

[17] Actually, this is not inconsistent with the Taylor results, which showed that intervention by these G3 central banks were loss-making but that the results were not statistically significant.

[18] I. M. Destler and C. Randall Henning, *Dollar Politics: Exchange Rate Policymaking in the United States* (Washington, D.C.: Institute for International Economics, 1989), 20; C.

Randall Henning, *Currencies and Politics in the United States, Germany, and Japan* (Washington, D.C.: Institute for International Economics, 1994): 272.

[19] *New York Times*, June 6, 1981. Pöhl's view of intervention is known to be somewhat more complex than this quote suggests. In a rare insider account, Lawson recalls as follows: "He was also extraordinarily volatile—at one moment a confirmed sceptic about intervention in the foreign exchange markets, for example, and a prominent advocate of it the next. (There may have been some consistency in this instance, however: he tended to favor intervention when the dollar was strong vis-à-vis the Deutschemark and to be philosophically opposed to it when the dollar was weak)." Nigel Lawson, *The View from No. 11: Memoirs of a Tory Radical* (London: Bantam Press, 1992): 662.

[20] *International Herald Tribune*, June 3, 1982; emphasis added.

[21] For the American results which emphasize the lack of evidence for effectiveness, see "Intervention in Foreign Exchange Markets: A Summary of Ten Staff Studies," *Federal Reserve Bulletin* 69, 11 (November 1983): 830-36. Case studies done by the Japanese government are more sympathetic to intervention and are summarized in Toyoo Gyohten, "Wagakunino Kawase Sijo Kainyu ni kansuru Kesu Sutadi, Jo, Ge (Case Studies on Japanese Intervention in Foreign Exchange Markets, Parts I and II)," *Finance: Ohkurasho Koho* 21, 4 (July 1985): 64-75; 21, 4 (August 1985): 49-58.

[22] *Report of the Working Group on Exchange Market Intervention* (Paris: La Documentation Française, 1983): 72.

[23] Ibid., 70.

[24] Ibid., 78.

[25] Nigel Lawson, Chancellor of the Exchequer, used Margaret Thatcher's close relationship with President Reagan to make this move possible. He writes: "Shortly before leaving for Washington on the afternoon of 16 January, I saw Margaret and told her I thought the G5 meeting would be an excellent opportunity to garner some international support for sterling. The principal obstacle I faced was the US Treasury Secretary, Donald Regan, who still adhered to the laissez-faire exchange rate policy of Reagan's first term. The best means of influencing him was to draw on Margaret's exceptionally close relationship with President Reagan, to whom Don Regan could be expected to defer. I drafted a letter for Margaret's signature on the worrying effects the excessively strong and seemingly ever-rising dollar was having on the pound, which after making a few amendments, she sent to the President." Lawson, *The View from No. 11*, 472-73.

[26] *New York Times*, January 18, 1985.

[27] *International Herald Tribune*, March 6, 1985.

[28] *U.S. News and World Report*, April 8, 1985, 28.

[29] Ibid.

[30] *International Herald Tribune*, March 22, 1985.

[31] *U.S. News and World Report*, April 8, 1985, 28.

[32] Martin Feldstein, "Correcting the Trade Deficit," *Foreign Affairs* 65, 2 (Spring 1987): 800.

[33] Ibid., 799.

[34] Richard Darman, *Who's in Control? Polar Politics and the Sensible Center* (New York: Simon and Schuster, 1996): 172.

[35] James A. Baker III, *The Politics of Diplomacy: Revolution, War and Peace 1989-1992* (New York: G.P. Putnam's Sons, 1995).

[36] Volcker and Gyohten, *Changing Fortunes*, 274.

[37] Volcker and Gyohten, *Changing Fortunes*, 234; Owen F. Humpage, "Institutional Aspect of U.S. Intervention," *Federal Reserve Bank of Cleveland Economic Review* 30, 1 (1994): 2-19.

Chapter 5

Conclusions

The only certainty is uncertainty.
Pliny the Elder, *Historia Naturalis*, 2: 7.

1.   INTRODUCTION

Chapters 1 and 2 developed four classes of theories of counterproductive cooperation, selectively drawing on the existing literature. The first class of theories, represented in particular by the Rogoff model, indicates that cooperation can be counterproductive when there is a third party, such as market agents, that is not directly involved. Specifically, the Rogoff model predicts that monetary cooperation exacerbates the inflationary bias of discretionary monetary policy.

The second class of theories argues that monetary policymakers may have noneconomic motives that lead them to engage in counterproductive cooperation. Cooperation may therefore be optimal for the policymakers but may not be beneficial for the economies involved. The Tabellini model, for example, shows that budget deficits could be larger under coordination when policymakers are myopic because of upcoming elections. Feldstein points to the tendency of politicians to blame central banks and foreigners because it is politically expedient to do so.

The third class of theories focuses on model uncertainty as a possible cause of counterproductive coordination. As forcefully argued by Frankel, if policymakers rely on highly imprecise economic models, there is no guarantee that cooperation will be successful. In such a situation, disagreement among policymakers from different countries becomes very likely or even inevitable, making it difficult to forge a consensus for coordination. If cooperation happens, policymakers can easily interpret the outcome to be counterproductive, and a negative lesson is learned as a result.

The fourth class of theories focuses on coercion as a possible source of counterproductive cooperation, at least from the point of view of the coerced. From this perspective, it is not surprising that the Japanese and Germans, who were subject to political pressure from the United States, often perceive cooperation to be counterproductive.

Chapter 3 then examined some statistical and qualitative evidence. There is some evidence that growth of the money supply is faster than average in periods of coordination periods (Figures 3-1 through 3-3 in Chapter 3), and that is consistent with the predictions of the Rogoff model. At the same time, however, the inflation rate and the misery index in the G3 countries are not visibly higher, compared with ordinary years. Thus, the statistical evidence is mixed.

The evidence is also ambiguous about the validity of the Tabellini model. Except for Japan, there is little evidence that budget deficits are significantly larger under coordination. And even in Japan, where the budget deficits in coordination years are larger than average, the evidence is not clear-cut.

There is ample evidence that model uncertainty existed in the episodes of G7 coordination. Schmidt and other German officials repeatedly questioned the economic scenario proposed by the Carter administration. The Bank of Japan was operating under considerable uncertainty about the proper course of monetary policy in the late 1980s, and by the time it realized that monetary policy overshot, the bubble economy was out of control.

It is appropriate to point out, however, that it is impossible to refute a realist critique that the talk of uncertainty is a thinly disguised veil covering over fundamental conflicts of interest. The burden is on these critics to prove that the German and Japanese as well as the American officials who proposed cooperative packages were certain about the economic consequences of various courses of action (and that there was a near consensus among their predictions).[1] Such evidence is very hard to come by.

There is some evidence for coercion, but it is not clear whether the use of the dollar weapon was premeditated in each of the cases. What is clear is that coercion is a recipe for distrust, which was ample in both periods examined in Chapter 3, and for long-term negative consequences.

Chapter 4 focused on another area of cooperation among the major industrial countries, namely, coordination of foreign exchange intervention. The chapter first summarized the arguments as to the ineffectiveness and counterproductivity of foreign exchange intervention. Dean Taylor, for example, argued that central banks destabilize the foreign exchange markets by selling low and buying high, thereby incurring huge losses in foreign exchange operations. The empirical data show that frequent coordination was concentrated in more or less the same period as those of fiscal and monetary policy coordination. This shows indirectly that even if foreign exchange intervention is sterilized and hence functionally separated from domestic monetary policy, there are still some loose links due to political factors. The chapter also showed some tests for Taylor's counterproductiveness thesis by examining whether the G3 central banks are selling high and buying low. The results are highly mixed, making it difficult to say that central bank intervention is systematically destabilizing, as Taylor had suggested. Finally, the case study of the intervention debate among the G7 governments in the 1980s highlights the existence of model uncertainty. Policymakers disagreed quite dramatically about the effectiveness and counterproductiveness of foreign exchange intervention: even as the Treasury officials in the Reagan administration argued tirelessly that intervention is ineffective and sometimes counterproductive, their European and Japanese counterparts disagreed. Such lack of consensus is not the most conducive environment for fruitful collaboration. It is therefore no surprise that the effectiveness of the Plaza Agreement and the subsequent attempts at exchange rate management is still a matter of dispute.

In conclusion, there is overall some evidence in favor of all of the theories of counterproductive cooperation, but the most robust one seems to be that of model uncertainty. It is simply impossible to make firm cause-effect inference about these highly contingent series of events. Thus, it remains a matter of controversy whether the Bonn summit had any contributory effect on the second oil crisis because there is no good economic model that can affirm such a link. In a similar vein, it is hard to know for certain to what extent the Plaza-Louvre agreements contributed to the bubble economy in Japan. Those who believe that they can prove these cause-effect relationships are surely deluding themselves. In this sense, then, the theory of model uncertainty is valid and "confirmed."

For those whose worldview is deterministic, this theory will be highly unsatisfactory. But to admit that there is this kind of uncertainty in international monetary cooperation has immense and rich policy implications, as will be clear shortly. Thus, to prove the certainty of model uncertainty is not the same as saying that there is nothing important we can say about this elusive phenomenon.

2. COOPERATION IN INTERNATIONAL LENDING OF LAST RESORT

I argued in Chapter 1 that international monetary cooperation among the major financial powers is worthy of study because of its normative significance: it is one of the few ways to assure a modicum of stability in the international financial system. I also argued that there are three main forms of cooperation among the G3 monetary authorities: monetary policy coordination, coordination of foreign exchange intervention, and cooperation in the international lender-of-last-resort functions.

Walter Bagehot had argued that in times of financial panic, the central bank should lend without limit (albeit at a penalty rate to safeguard against moral hazard) until the panic subsides. The international monetary system lacks a world central bank or world currency and hence it is impossible for anyone to extend that kind of international credit. This is the theoretical basis of Kindleberger's hegemonic stability theory; indeed, the central bank of a hegemonic country may have sufficient capability to assist other nations in trouble. Given that such hegemony does not exist today, cooperation among the major economic powers such as the United States, Japan, and Germany is crucial for fending off a potential worldwide meltdown of the financial system.

Cooperation in international lending of last resort is a vast subject itself and would require its own volume to do it justice. Also, aside from the critique of IMF conditionality,[2] it is hard to find a systematic theory of counterproductive cooperation in this area. For these reasons, it has been left out of the scope of this book. But the findings of this book have some important implications for this area of international monetary cooperation among the G3.

First, money lent from the IMF and the major creditor nations is often used for intervention in foreign exchange markets by the borrowing governments because their currencies are under speculative attack. Thus, the ineffectiveness and counterproductiveness theses about foreign exchange intervention are relevant. If policymakers in creditor countries strongly believe that such use of international borrowing is wasted through intervention, they may refuse to lend to the country contemplating such intervention. As in the case of coordination of foreign exchange intervention, the theory of counterproductive intervention has powerful implications for international monetary cooperation in this area as well.

Also, there is some talk of monetary policy coordination among the Asian countries, along with a proposal for establishment of an Asian IMF, which Robert Rubin rejected out of hand. Indeed, while monetary tightening makes some sense if only one country is in financial crisis because it will attract foreign capital as well as contract imports, simultaneous tightening of monetary policy by all the countries in a region makes less sense, since that would trigger a scramble for foot-loose capital. As a result, all the countries will contract their economies too much. Indeed, that is what happened in Asia in 1997 as a result of the IMF's imposing conditionality simultaneously on Thailand, Indonesia, and Korea. In light of this, there will be more talk about monetary policy coordination in Asia in the aftermath of this crisis, and the theory of counterproductiveness of monetary policy coordination then becomes relevant.

Finally, there is a link between counterproductiveness of monetary cooperation and cooperation in international lending of last resort. Bitter experience with coordination in one functional area may spill over to other areas. Even though foreign exchange intervention and domestic monetary policy are "separate" functional areas, chapters 3 and 4 show that the cycles of cooperation in the two areas coincide. Similarly, cooperation in international crisis rescue operations may also correlate with coordination of other policy instruments. The experience of the 1930s, when cooperation broke down across the board (not only in monetary issues but also trade cooperation), does not give us grounds for optimism in this regard.[3]

3. POLICY RECOMMENDATIONS

3.1. Need for more research on uncertainty

The single most important policy implication of the findings of this book—the validity of model uncertainty—is that policymakers should take this issue more seriously and put more energy, time, and money into researching the issue. Research on model uncertainty was conducted mostly in academia and think tanks such as the Brookings Institution and the Centre for Economic Policy Research in London in the 1980s.[4] But with the decline in policy interest in monetary coordination, this research program languished very quickly in the 1990s. This is unfortunate. Without prejudging whether monetary cooperation is beneficial, there is a need for more research, debate, and thinking among policymakers on a less technical and quantitative level with some input from academic and think-tank analyses.

3.2. Need for contingency planning

After some thinking and brainstorming about uncertainty, the next obvious step will be to plan ahead. Consider the example of business. Businesses explicitly take risk into account in preparing for all sorts of contingencies and scenarios when they develop new products or embark on new ventures.[5] Policymakers should take a lesson from this method, because policy without a contingency plan is never likely to succeed, given the risk involved. When they conceive of international cooperation, they should never assume that it will work perfectly or conversely that it will be disastrous. All contingencies are possible with some degree of likelihood. The key is to have a plan for each of these scenarios.

3.3. Hedge or diversify the policy portfolio

Another way business copes with risk is through hedging and diversification. Of course, business is more privileged in having a number of financial instruments it can simply buy on the market to hedge against risks. Policymakers do not have the luxury of such financial instruments to hedge against the adverse consequences of policy errors. Perhaps, portfolio diversification may be a better analogy. International monetary cooperation in some cases may look promising, but never put all your trust in it; things could always go wrong; blaming foreigners may be an easy way out (at least in the short run), but it is never a fundamental solution. Policymakers should start thinking about policy instruments like separate financial instruments in a portfolio. It is rare today, for instance, for strategic thinkers to think of different policy instruments in this way. Different policy instruments have different combinations of payoffs under different contingencies; combining them in an imaginative way may go a long way in hedging against some policy errors.

3.4. Need for training for coping with uncertainty

Uncertainty is a hard concept to grasp. It is known, for instance, that people instinctively overestimate small-probability events.[6] Another common hubris is that people tend to have excessive confidence about their probability estimates.[7] These cognitive biases are firmly established in psychology, and it is probably correct to assume that monetary policymakers suffer from these biases as well. Psychologists also have some methods to counteract some of these cognitive biases under uncertainty. Thus, it is highly recommendable that monetary policymakers get some training about how to assess uncertain events.

3.5. Give cooperation a chance

Finally, I fear that the theme of this book—risk involved in international monetary cooperation—may have an undue restraining effect on policymakers. One of the virtues of excellent leadership is courage in the face of crisis and challenge. It is no coincidence that great presidents are often associated with great crises. Thus, Abraham Lincoln in the Civil War and Franklin D. Roosevelt in the Great Depression and World War II. The last thing I would wish from world government leaders is to recoil in the face of uncertainty. It is true that monetary cooperation is risky; but if the consequences, economic and political, of inaction are immense, leaders should not hesitate to give cooperation a chance.

NOTES

[1] It could happen that some of them were very certain about their forecasts, but due to the problem of overconfidence (to be mentioned below), that is not enough to prove that model uncertainty did not exist.

[2] International lending of last resort is usually done multilaterally through standby credit facilities of the International Monetary Fund. In granting standby loans, it is customary for the IMF to impose a set of policy prescriptions, known as conditionality, on the borrowing nation. The specific contents of IMF conditionality are highly contested. For instance, Jeffrey Sachs argued that the IMF imposed monetary tightening on Korea but that it was highly inappropriate for a country already suffering from price deflation. Jeffrey Sachs, "IMF is a Power unto Itself," *Financial Times*, December 11, 1997. It is also reported that the IMF's prescription to shut down dozens of financial institutions in Indonesia caused more uncertainty and a run.

[3] Optimists would have to argue that cooperation in different functional areas would happen independently of each other.

[4] Ralph C. Bryant, *International Coordination of National Stabilization Policies* (Washington, D.C.: Brookings, 1995); Ralph C. Bryant, David A. Currie, Jacob A. Frenkel, Paul Masson, and Richard Portes, eds., *Macroeconomic Policies in an Interdependent World* (Washington, D.C.: Brookings, 1989); Ralph C. Bryant *et al*, *Empirical Macroeconomics for Interdependent Economies* (Washington, D.C.: Brookings, 1988); Ralph C. Bryant and Richard Portes, eds., *Global Macroeconomics: Policy Conflict and Cooperation* (London: Macmillan Press, 1987); Marjorie Deane and Robert Pringle, *Economic Cooperation from the Inside* (New York: Group of Thirty, 1984); Wilfried Guth, ed., *Economic Policy Coordination* (Washington, D.C.: International Monetary Fund, 1988); The Group of Thirty, *International Macroeconomic Policy Coordination* (New York and London: Group of Thirty, 1988); Gerald Holtham, *International Policy Coordination: How Much Consensus is There?*, Brookings Discussion Papers on International Economics 50 (September 1986); Gerald Holtham and Andrew Hughes Hallett, "International Policy Cooperation and Model Uncertainty," in Ralph Bryant and Richard Portes, eds., *Global Macroeconomics: Policy Conflict and Cooperation* (Houndmills, Hampshire: Macmillan, 1987); Patrick Minford and Matthew Canzoneri, *Policy Interdependence: Does Strategic Behavior Pay? An Empirical Investigation Using the Liverpool World Model*, Centre for Economic Policy Research Discussion Paper 201 (October 1987); Gilles Oudiz and Jeffrey Sachs, "Macroeconomic Policy Coordination among the Industrial Economies," *Brookings Papers on Economic Activity* 1 (1984): 1-75; Jacques J. Polak, *Coordination of National Economic Policies*, Occasional Papers 7 (New York: Group of Thirty, 1981); Paul A. Volcker *et al*, *International Monetary Cooperation: Essays in Honor of Henry C. Wallich*, Essays in International Finance 169 (Princeton: International Finance Section, Department of Economics, Princeton University, December 1987). For more academic treatment in the

1980s, see William H. Branson, Jacob A. Frenkel, and Morris Goldstein, eds., *International Policy Coordination and Exchange Rate Fluctuations* (Chicago: University of Chicago Press, 1990); Willem H. Buiter and Richard C. Marston, eds., *International Economic Policy Coordination* (Cambridge: Cambridge University Press, 1985); Richard N. Cooper, "Economic Interdependencies and Coordination of Policy," In Ronald Jones and Peter Kenen, eds., *Handbook of International Economics* Vol. 2. (Amsterdam: North-Holland, 1985); Martin Feldstein, ed., *International Economic Cooperation* (Chicago: University of Chicago Press, 1988); Peter B. Kenen, *Exchange Rates and Policy Coordination* (Ann Arbor: University of Michigan Press, 1989).

[5] Jeffry A. Timmons, "The Business Plan," in John Leslie Livingston, ed., *The Portable MBA in Finance and Accounting*, 2nd ed. (New York: Wiley, 1997): 274-77.

[6] M. Granger Morgan and Max Henrion, *Uncertainty: A Guide to Dealing with Uncertainty in Quantitative Risk and Policy Analysis* (Cambridge: Cambridge University Press, 1990): 103-04.

[7] Ibid., 116.

Index